JAMES STEPHENS: A CRITICAL STUDY

Augustine Martin

JAMES STEPHENS: A CRITICAL STUDY

ROWMAN AND LITTLEFIELD

TOTOWA, NEW JERSEY

First published in the United States 1977
by Rowman and Littlefield, Totowa, N.J.

© Augustine Martin 1977

Library of Congress Cataloging in Publication Data

Martin, Augustine.
    James Stephens, a critical study.
    Bibliography : pp. 4
    Includes index.
    1. Stephens, James, 1882–1950
    Criticism and interpretation.   I.   Title.
PR6037 . T4Z78   1977   821' . 9'12   77–3915
ISBN 0–87471–968–2

Grateful acknowledgment is made to the following for permission
to reproduce copyright material : Macmillan Publishing Co. Inc.
for extracts from *The Letters of James Stephens* edited by Richard
J. Finnernan; *In the Land of Youth* by James Stephens, © 1924 by
Macmillan Publishing Co. Inc., renewed 1952 by Cynthia Stephens;
Songs from the Clay by James Stephens, © 1915 by Macmillan
Publishing Co. Inc., renewed 1943 by James Stephens; *Collected
Poems* of James Stephens, © 1954 by Macmillan Publishing Co.
Inc;. and also to The Society of Authors as the literary representa-
tive of the Estate of James Stephens for extracts from *The Demi-
Gods* by James Stephens.

Printed in Great Britain

To my Mother
and in memory of my Father

*To my Mother
and in memory of my Father*

Contents

Preface

Few books of such modest scope as this can boast of such a large list of benefactors. My enthusiasm for the work of James Stephens was first stimulated by the lectures of Professor Roger McHugh at University College Dublin more than twenty years ago, and by the lectures of Dr Richard Walsh on Stephens's merit as a translator from the Irish. I must thank Professor Richard Carey of the *Colby Library Quarterly*, Mr James Delehanty of *The Kilkenny Magazine* and Father Roland Burke-Savage of *Studies* for publishing my early efforts of criticism of Stephens's poetry, prose and translations.

My debts to Dr Birgit Bramsbäck for her pioneering work in Stephens bibliography and to Professor Richard Finneran for his magisterial edition of the letters are everywhere apparent in the pages that follow. My thanks for critical guidance are due to Professor Denis Donoghue, Professor Proinsias Mac Cana and Dr Seamus Deane at U.C.D. In the matter of style and organisation I am grateful to Miss Marlene Hackett who saw the book through its final drafts.

My gratitude is due to Mrs Veronica McCarthy, Leitrim County Librarian, for providing me at an early stage with copies of Stephens's more inaccessible publications. For early advice, encouragement and assistance I am indebted to Father Denis Ryan and Mrs Breda McCormack. Finally I must acknowledge the patience of my wife Claire in putting up with me during the tedious years of the book's gestation. I need hardly add that while much of the book's merit, such as it is, is due to my friends, its shortcomings are solely my responsibility.

Augustine Martin,
University College Dublin, 1977.

Introduction

James Stephens, in an essay published in 1914, asserts that 'no person should write biography but a competent critic', and goes on to insist that such a biographer 'should not avail himself of letters or anecdotes about the person he is celebrating. His psychological analysis should be entirely based on the published works ... and his aim should be to release from the stories the character which is entangled on every page of them.'[1] Thirty-five years later, in a radio talk on Yeats, he came back to the same theme :

> There is the poet and the poetry. The one so ordinary, the other actually so incalculable. How these two ever got together is a mystery. There is the Milton who composed and the Milton who didn't. How enriched we should be if we knew nothing about Milton except what we know about Homer; that both were blind, and they both had dazzling insight; and as to their three meals a day and a job, who cares![2]

The present book at least compromises with these prescriptions. It is a study of the work, not of the life or the legend. And it has its source in the conviction that the work, especially the prose, has been too long obscured by the remembered personality of its begetter.

When Stephens died in London in January 1951, he was best known for his brilliant, whimsical broadcasts on the B.B.C. There, week after week, he continued to project the curious personality that had so beguiled Dublin in the early years of the century, and that had enchanted America in the decades that followed. It was as author of *The Crock of Gold* that he was first most universally acclaimed; and the resemblance between the author and his fictional creations seemed to abolish all hope of

x *Introduction*

more serious critical considerations. Diminutive in stature, puckered of countenance, divertingly garrulous—he was described as one of the 'three giants of Dublin talk'—he looked as if he had somehow invented himself : the loquacity of his Philosopher fused to the physique and mischief of his leprecauns. He seemed like a fey emanation of the Celtic Twilight as it flickered to a close in the light of the twentieth century. He cultivated this image of himself in a variety of ways, and became in a sense its victim. Since his death he tends to be remembered for a handful of light lyrics in the anthologies—though his *Collected Poems* has never gone out of print—and *The Crock of Gold*. His lifetime of strenuous experiment, especially with prose fiction, has virtually been forgotten, lost behind the shimmer of that admittedly brilliant fantasy.

Stephens was notoriously secretive about his parentage and the circumstances of his early childhood. The date of his birth is still a matter of dispute and conjecture. The stories that he told of his boyhood have the flavour of fantasy, and they may well have been invented to deflect curiosity from the facts, if he knew them, or from their absence, if he did not. The stories tell how he worked for a time as a clown in a circus; how he made the journey from Dublin to Belfast on foot; how he found work driving a horse and cart and had to climb on a box every time he harnessed and unharnessed the beast because of his smallness; how he slept on park benches and once fought a swan for a crust of bread; how he was rescued from starvation by a kindly prostitute but was impelled to leave her room when he realised that he was depriving her of a living by his presence there. His lavishness with these romantic anecdotes is matched by his reticence in the face of any formal request for hard information. His reply to a correspondent in 1914 is typical of his attitude : 'I am the proprietor of a past that could not stir the heart of the great American nation. It is tame, it is hygienic, let me hasten to forget it. Unlike Jesus Christ I was born with the aid of a father as well as a mother. I will stir these ashes no more or I may discover other lapses from the tradition of true greatness.'[3] Whatever his motives Stephens had remarkable success in substituting childhood legend for biographical fact. His two biographers, Birgit Bramsbäck and Hilary Pyle have not succeeded in plucking out the heart of the mystery. Dr Bramsbäck at the end of her extensive researches concludes that 'one may even have to reckon with the possibility that James Stephens is an assumed name'.[4] Miss Pyle claims to have solved the problem of his birth and parentage by identifying him as the 'unnamed boy child' born on 8 February 1880, to Francis Stephens of Her Majesty's Stationery Office, Dublin.[5] Richard Finneran, having worked for several years on his admirable *Collected Letters*, finds himself unable to make 'a firm choice' as between the possible alternatives. For the purpose of this study the date given by Stephens himself, 2 February 1882—Joyce's birthday—is adopted as being the most likely.

The facts that have been established suggest a life far more conventional and humdrum than that pictured in the romantic legends. He was a boarder at the Meath Protestant Industrial School for Boys between 1886 and 1896. On leaving he was employed by a Dublin solicitor named Wallace, and in the years that followed he found employment in a succession of such legal offices. When George Russell, AE, called on him in 1907—he had read some of Stephens's pieces in *Sinn Féin*—he found him behind a desk in the office of T. T. Mecredy and Sons of Merrion Square.

But while the stories of vagrancy and adventure may be useless to the biographer they probably contain a valuable hint for the student of the writings. One has only to read an early poem such as 'Fifty Pounds a Year and a Pension' to sense how Stephens hated the routine and constriction of his working life, 'Totting little lines of figures'. In an interview given to *Time* in 1951 he remarked : 'I thought in those days that I'd be a poet. All day I used to sit and think of big words. By big I mean fine-sounding words like "honor" and "noble" and "courage" and I spent my time writing them down.' It is possible that the childhood legend was created in response to a similar need. The world he had been forced by circumstances to inhabit was unendurably squalid and tedious and the author created in his imagination a sort of counter truth, a world of drama, pathos and romance to replace it. In an essay of 1924 Stephens had described his creative impulse as his 'desire-nature' : 'In every book it is the author that is the real subject. The story he is telling is his own choice. And in considering it we are investigating one true aspect of the author in his desire-nature.'[6] I suspect that this phrase is the key to much of his writing. In the early poetry and in such a later story as 'Hunger' Stephens reveals himself as a bitter critic of the social conditions in which contemporary man is forced to live. And it is clear that his bitterness has roots in his personal experience of Dublin's streets, offices and tenements. But in much of his work, even when as in *The Charwoman's Daughter* he is portraying these conditions, this bitterness is in abeyance. This is the case when his imagination, his 'desire-nature' is at work in creating for itself a better world, as in *The Crock of Gold* where he creates that idyllic 'country of the Gods'. The process has, as I hope to show, nothing, or very little, to do with simple 'escapism'. It has a great deal more to do with the doctrine of Blake—the first major influence on Stephens's thought—that the purpose of art is to bring back the Golden Age. In a letter to John Drinkwater in 1917 Stephens makes his case for the imagination in these forthright terms:

> I believe that everything the best mind of humanity really wishes for, and formulates the wish, must come to pass. So I look on certain abstract words such as 'love', 'honour', 'spirit' as prophetic words, having no concrete existence now, but to be forged in the future by the desire which has sounded them. Poems, too, are to me prophesies, and there will be a gay old world sometime.[7]

From the start and throughout his life Stephens was exercised by the gap that exists between the reality that man is given and must with his physical body endure, and the world that he aspires to in his reveries and seeks to make real through imagination. It is out of this tension that Stephens's work is shaped, the tension between 'things as they are' and things as they might become through the exertion of our desire-nature. It is in his first prose fiction, *The Charwoman's Daughter*, that this dialogue between actuality and dream becomes most clearly articulate.

The Charwoman's Daughter

Fairy Tale and Novel of Growth

Before its publication in book form in 1912 *The Charwoman's Daughter* ran as a serial in *The Irish Review* between April 1911 and February 1912 under the title, *Mary, A Story*. The American edition came out in 1912 under the title, *Mary, Mary*. It was Stephens's most triumphant year of publication with his second volume of poems, *The Hill of Vision, The Crock of Gold* and this, his first novel, appearing within the same twelve months.

The Charwoman's Daughter is a most original book not because it was the first novel to describe life in Dublin's slums but because in it Stephens manages to convey such a complex vision of human psychology within the frame and morphology of the oldest and simplest of narrative forms, the fairy tale. In harnessing the fairy tale to the conditions of the Dublin tenements Stephens is at once overt and subtle. His heroine, his Cinderella, is introduced as Mary Makebelieve, thus stressing from the outset the fabulous character and contour of the fiction. It is her condition to live among the cinders and to dream, urged on by her mother, of a better world. This world is frankly named at the opening of Chapter 3 as 'that somewhere which is the country of Romance'. With a symmetry which would satisfy Vladimir Propp's most classic formulations she proceeds through vicissitude, error and hazard to the final goal of wealth, health and the promise of successful marriage. She outwits the ogre, in the form of the policeman, the ogress, in the person of his aunt, and the dangers of the threatening landscape, the perilous city of adult experience. The posture of her dreams is in harmony with the class conventions of the fairy tale and its more literary counterpart, the romantic comedy. The dreams of matrimony which she and her mother harbour 'could only concentrate on the person of a lord'. The policeman, the first focus of her unconscious erotic impulse, is lordly with 'his calm, proud eye—a governing, compelling, and determined eye'. In this first, and as it turns out, false, transmogrification of fantasy into reality the fabulous and the real mesh in a manner characteristic of the novel. It is a novel which brings the literary form—fairy tale, romance, romantic comedy—into questioning relationship with life as it is lived, and does so as consciously as *Northanger Abbey* interrogates the Gothick romance in the court of quotidian experience. It is in that sense a book about writing a book and might fruitfully be compared with the reflexive fictions of such writers as John Fowles, Robert Coover, John Barth and Flann O'Brien and perhaps the father of such fictions, the author of *Tristram Shandy*. Its self-conscious designs on us are however so subtly woven into the unfolding narrative that it is only in retrospect that we see the full sophistication of its design. A similar 'narrative charm'—to use the usual dismissive formula—has bedevilled criticism of *The Crock of Gold*, consigning Stephens to the realm of children's wonder-tales, an Irish response to Kenneth Grahame.

The Charwoman's Daughter is a novel about growing up. This process is presented as complex and many-faceted. The young heroine must fight her way, however unconsciously at first, out of the unreal and makebelieve world of her mother's possessive fantasies. She must encounter the challenge of sexuality, enter the arena where man and woman meet, and come to terms with a new and radical version of human possessiveness. She must confront the realities of class as they exist in the real world and bring these realities to bear on the fantasies of class distinction which are sponsored by her dalliance in the 'country of Romance'. She must learn to relate the private world of her poverty in the tenement to the universal implications of poverty as they collide with the world of plenty and privilege in the Dublin of Mrs O'Connor's bourgeois establishment, of the streets, its carriages, theatres and restaurants. These are the processes of maturation through which the heroine must proceed. The triumph of the novel is the manner in which these ordeals of learning and development are dramatised truthfully, painfully and convincingly.

Her mother creates for Mary a world of vivid possibility amidst the deprivation and squalor of their tenement. We learn little about Mrs Makebelieve's past except that she has known better days. She recalls for her daughter a husband, Mary's father, but a doubt hovers over that relationship. What is clear is that neither must look to him for comfort or advancement. Whatever hope of rescue exists is focused on Mary's uncle Patrick whose expected aid is invoked in Chapter 6, Chapter 12 and Chapter 20 where he is envisioned by the mother in an actual dream 'wherein she saw her brother Patrick standing on the remotest sea point of distant America, from whence he shouted loudly across the ocean that he was coming back to Ireland soon, that he had succeeded very well indeed, and that he was not married'.[1] The *données* of Mary's initial situation are therefore a continuation of her poverty, the emotional confinement of her mother's possessive love, the consolation of impossible romantic fantasies, the hardly more possible supervention of a fairy uncle from America—that perennial resource of Irish fiction writers.

The limitation of Mary's emotional horizons is subtly dramatised in her daily wanderings round the city while her mother is at work, specifically in her visits to St Stephen's Green. Here, as she dreamily watches the birds in the duckpond, the only relation she can conceive is the maternal. She differentiates between the ducks 'that had chickens, and those that had had chickens, and those that never had any chickens at all'. These, we are told, 'were usually drakes' and therefore 'did not deserve the pity which Mary lavished on their childlessness'. When she sees the eels move through the water with unusual speed 'Mary Makebelieve thought that the latter kind had just heard their babies crying' and wondered 'could its mother see the tears where there was already so much water about'. Already sixteen and poised on the brink of womanhood—the stage at which Stephens so often introduces his fictional heroines—she does not as yet 'understand the basic necessity which drives the male to the female'. Her mother has ensured that the sexual urge is encased in the distancing glamour of romance and mystery.

Within the process of the novel she is to experience the sensation and the reality before they have been explained to her. The occasion is her contemplation of the great policeman directing traffic at the junction of Suffolk Street and Grafton Street, and in Stephens's prose the moment is charged with drama :

The figure of the massive policeman fascinated her. Surely everything desirable in manhood was concentrated in his tremendous body. What an immense, shattering blow that mighty fist could give. She could imagine it swinging vast as the buffet of an hero, high-thrown and then down irresistibly—a crashing, monumental hand. She delighted in his great, solid head as it swung slowly from side to side, and his calm, proud eye— a governing, commanding and determined eye.[2]

His presentation is in subtle accord with the knightly aura of the mother's imaginary suitors. But it is also shot through with something new, a sense of alien, masculine strength and a slightly menacing suggestion of power. When her eyes meet his, this latter suggestion becomes dangerously overt : 'One day her shy, creeping glance caught his; it held her mesmerised for a few seconds; it looked down into her—for a moment the whole world seemed to have become one immense eye—she could hardly get away from it.' She makes her way home with 'a queer, frightened exaltation lightening through her blood'. She has moved from the dream into the reality, and from the exclusive world of woman into the world of men and women.

Within the imaginative schema of the novel St Stephen's Green and the Phoenix Park represent two separate areas of experience. The Green has been Mary's world of childhood reverie. It is in the Park that she first encounters the policeman. He comes upon her from behind, and when he seats himself beside her she feels with a more palpable force the sense of his enormous maleness, the attraction and the dread which it constitutes for her inexperienced womanhood. She is 'almost mesmerised by the huge tweed-clad knees that towered like monoliths beside her' and is reminded in a telling phrase of 'the immovable knees of a god which she had once seen in the museum'. His attitude to her is godlike in its omniscience and condescension as he explains 'the more unusual and learned words that bristled from his vocabulary' and interprets her awe-struck silence as 'the natural homage of a girl to a policeman'.[3] From this point on, Mary begins to live a double life. She senses the incompatability of the new relationship with the old one of mother and child, feels the abrasion of reality upon the fantasy life they had cultivated. Thus her change of direction at O'Connell Bridge in Chapter 12 is subtly symbolic: 'She said to herself with determined candour that she would walk up to St Stephen's Green Park and look at the ducks and the flower beds and the eels, but when she reached the quays she blushed deeply, and turning towards the right, went rapidly in the direction of the Phoenix Park.' In that moment the world of childhood with its soft familial relationships is dramatically abandoned and the challenge of adult experience taken up.

The Ordeal of Class

The rhetoric of the fairy tale depends on class structures genially organised to secure the heroine's final elevation and happiness. Part of Mary's maturation involves her discovery that the class structures of her city are ugly, unjust and humiliating. The policeman in his bland interrogations keeps returning to her mother's 'business'.

By the end of Chapter 13 she finds herself faced by the fact that 'she could not bear to say that her mother was a charwoman'. When the question can no longer be evaded 'Mary Makebelieve told him a lie. She said her mother was a dressmaker.' Her sense of shame grows more intense and palpable when it is provoked on her own behalf in that brilliant passage of Chapter 18 where the policeman enters the O'Connor hallway and finds Mary on her knees scrubbing the floor. The naïvety of the Cinderella myth is deftly reversed when he 'hung his monstrous gaze upon her' and then turned to his aunt as if she did not exist. This nadir of Mary's social humiliation provides her with a flash of insight that proves ultimately redemptive. She begins to sense an unpleasant shift in the policeman's attitude : 'he now condescended from the loftiness of a policeman and a person of quality to the quaint gutters of social inferiority . . . and since the policeman had discovered Mary publicly washing out an alien hall his respect for her had withered and dropped to death almost in an instant'. It is here, in Chapter 24, that she finds within herself the resources of instinct, intelligence and character to reject him. The theme of sexual growth, so far subtly and tinglingly present in the fable, becomes explicit and salient.

Man and Woman

The struggle between Mary and the policeman is a struggle of polar opposites. In his poetry Stephens appropriated the Theosophist doctrine of a universe energised by the conflict of warring antinomies, good and evil, light and darkness, night and day, man and woman. Here Mary is presented as radically feminine. She has exclusively inhabited a woman's world in which the 'mother-spirit' sponsors values of solicitude, tenderness and domesticity. The policeman, on the other hand, is schematically presented as embodying the masculine principle at its most aggressive. He is large, muscular, commanding, god-like, proprietorial. In the early phases of the novel these qualities are softened by the point of view. Through the heroine's awe-struck and inexperienced consciousness they take on the romance and glamour of the unknown. They represent all the strange male forces from which her mother, by many devices, has shielded her. They present a challenge which her nascent sexuality impels her to encounter.

But we are not unprepared. Before the policeman had entered the story, at the end of Chapter 3, Mary had been caught in a startlingly Lawrentian fantasy of the sexes:

> There was an attraction about young men which she could not understand, something peculiarly dear and magnetic; she would have liked to shake hands with one to see how different he felt from a girl. They would probably shake hands quite hard and then hit one. She fancied she would not mind being hit by a man, and then watching the vigour of their movements, she thought they hit very hard, but still there was a terrible attraction in the idea of being hit by a man.

She had asked her mother whether she had ever been struck by a man and her mother had been driven into a passion of grief in which Mary had found herself 'rocked fiercely against a heart bursting with bitter pride and recollection'. The question had remained unanswered as far as Mary had been concerned, but for the reader the word 'pride' has a telling resonance.

This incident comes to mind when Mary, in the next chapter, finds herself imagining what a 'shattering blow' the policeman's fist might deliver. And the emphasis is reinforced when, on their first encounter in the Park, she contemplates the same enormous hand in close-up: 'The specific gravity of that hand seemed tremendous. She could imagine it holding the strong neck of a bull. It moved continually while he spoke to her, closing in a tense strong grip that changed the mahogany colour to a dull whiteness, and opening again to a ponderous, inert width.' Beneath the comic surface of the narrative this Freudian, or more correctly, Lawrentian sense of sexual implication, together with the sense of archetypal male/female polarity, is persistently active. The girl is all delicacy, passivity and repressed fascination, the man radiates strength, dominance, male possessiveness. The drama issues from the heroine's eagerness to encounter what she barely comprehends, and from the reader's sense of her vulnerability, of the incongruity of the relation, the unevenness of the match.

It is, ironically, the social concern that proves Mary's salvation, that defines the limitations of the policeman's attraction and attractiveness. After the incident in the hallway and the shift in his attitude to her she becomes aware of being cultivated as an object of prey. The female archetype in her is alerted. She sees the predatory and proprietorial aspect of his attentions in a new angle of clarity. She recalls that 'he had always come from behind her', that 'his approach was always too policemanlike', that 'his advent hinted of a gross espionage'. Chapter 24 dramatises the process of disenchantment and brings to the surface the sexual reality so far masked by sentimentality and pretence. As they walk by the Dodder she perceives that in his addresses to her the 'gentleman' has been elided and only 'the man of the world' remains. His compliments ring hollow, 'she could see him making the things up as he talked'. Suddenly he appears no longer superb, just grossly 'big.' His eagerness suffers a shift in focus: 'it was greediness: he wanted to eat her up and go away with her bones sticking out of his mouth as the horns of a deer protrude from the jaws of an anaconda, veritable evidence to its fellows of a victory and an orgy to command respect and envy'. His increasingly familiar attentions become repellent: 'He did not keep his arms quiet, but tapped his remarks into her blouse and her shoulder. Each time his hands touched her they remained a trifle longer. They seemed to be great red spiders, they would grip her all round and squeeze her clammily while his face spiked her to death on his moustache . . .' He tries to take her by force and she escapes. The effectiveness of the scene derives from the counterpoint of Mary's internal monologue of distaste with the policeman's gross and uncomprehending effort of seduction. He is unaware that any change has taken place and he appears to the reader like any clownish and conventional seducer—Joyce's Corley without the latter's instinct for the timely occasion and the right victim. It is equally clear to the reader that Mary has come through her ordeal triumphantly, has done it alone, and in doing it has grown into a secure sense of her womanhood.

The policeman's subsequent adventures are a pattern of thwarted male power. Mary's rejection of him has 'injected a virus in his blood which was one-half a passion for her body and one-half a frenzy for vengeance'. The violence and strength which Mary had early seen in terms of romantic wonder have become an impotent ferocity which appears at once sinister and comic: 'He would gladly have beaten her into submission, for what right has a slip of a girl to withstand the advances of a policeman? That is a crooked spirit demanding to be straightened out with a truncheon.' When later he presents himself at the Makebelieve tenement and is finally rejected he 'could have smashed Mrs Makebelieve where she stood'. His final and squalid satisfaction is to batter the young clerk who has replaced him in the heroine's affections.

The logic of Stephens's view of the sexual has therefore worked its way inexorably through in the novel's process. The policeman has gone about his courting in the idiom of power and possessiveness. He has elaborately offended against the female principle which demands humility and submission before yielding itself totally in return. And the logic, though rigorously schematic in its working out, has been deftly accommodated to a fictional form where character and motivation are managed with a highly convincing sense of the spontaneous and a vivid sense of the actuality of time and place together with a remarkable precision of psychological insight.

Mother and Daughter

The public world of the novel concerns the struggle of Mary with the policeman. This area of its action takes place mostly out of doors. Her struggle with her mother provides the novel's inner or private action, and it takes place exclusively in the tenement. It is no less tense and in many respects is more gripping than the drama of the parks and the streets. In his one published comment on the book Stephens declares that he found the model for Mary in his wife, and that he looked within himself and 'found immediately my Charwoman',[4] which may account for the striking intensity of her realised character.

One aspect of Mary's growing up involves her escape from the charwoman's tightly woven net of fantasy and wishful thinking and into the world of real or everyday experience. The other side of the process resides in her cultivation of a life outside, which she must keep in guilty concealment from her mother. Her growth to womanhood entails the loss of innocence in more than one sense. It involves lies, pretence, actual treachery, and their attendant pain for a nature instinctively truthful and spontaneous. The main stages of the process are readily charted.

In the book's early phases life within the Makebelieve tenement is marked by certain rituals of continuity. The daughter wanders during the day while the mother goes to work. They exchange confidences in the mornings and the evenings. At night Mary does the talking as her mother is tired; she recounts the day's adventures in exhaustive detail. In the morning the mother, refreshed, carries the burden of the conversation, rehearsing for Mary the minutiae of the previous day's work. There is no concealment on either side or need of any.

When she comes home from her first encounter with the policeman Mary, who has never before kept a secret from her mother, is 'unable to tell her this one'. Instead she inquires about the desirability of policemen as husbands and is treated to a finely comic, and prophetic, discourse on the subject in which it is stressed that policemen 'thought too much of themselves, and their continual pursuit of and intercourse with criminals tended to deteriorate their moral tone' and that 'all things considered, a clerk made a better husband'. This is the only time when the public and private actions of the novel touch before their dramatic convergence in Chapter 24 when the policeman comes to the tenement to ask for Mary's hand.

By Chapter 15 Mary is in the grip of her romantic obsession almost to the extent of losing control of her will. Her mother is desperately ill and Mary goes out to buy her necessary provisions with the few pence they have left. Following a pattern we have glanced at earlier she turns at O'Connell Bridge and embarks on a hopeless search of the Park for her lover. The charwoman's illness is virtually banished from her mind and recurs only as a guilty and resented distraction from the real business of her emotions : 'A moment's reflection and she could have hated her mother.' She is rescued from reproach, if not from guilt, by the fact that her mother has been asleep through the long hours of her absence.

A moment of pathos and irony occurs at the end of Chapter 16 when poverty and sickness force the charwoman to send her daughter out to work :

> . . . for she saw in this work a beginning and an end—the end of a little daughter who could be petted and rocked and advised; the beginning of a womanhood which would grow up to and beyond her, which would collect and secrete emotions and aspirations and adventures not to be shared even by a mother; and she saw the failure which this work meant, the expanding of her daughter's life ripples to a bleak and miserable horizon where the clouds were soap-suds and floor-cloths, and the beyond a blank resignation only made energetic by hunger.

The pathos needs no annotation; it is especially evident in the less selfish part of the mother's anxiety, her vision of hunger, drudgery and humiliation. The irony is manifold in the account of the beginning of Mary's womanhood, of those new aspirations and adventures which she cannot share with her mother. The wreck of those aspirations is to be amid the soapsuds of the O'Connor household where she is being sent to work; in an incident where the social, familial and erotic themes of the novel momentarily converge.

The next convergence also takes place in the O'Connor household where the policeman tactlessly interrogates the charwoman on the subject of her daughter and is rewarded with a ferocious upsurge of Mrs Makebelieve's social resentment :

> ' "You're not in Court now, you jackanapes you," said I— with his whiskers, and his baton, and his feet that were bigger than anything in the world except his ignorant self-conceit. "Have you a daughter, ma'am?" said he. "What's her age, ma'am," said he. "Is she a good girl, ma'am?" said he.' But she had settled him. 'And that woman was prouder of him than a king would be of his crown! Never mind,' said Mrs Make-

believe, and she darted fiercely up and down the room, tearing pieces out of the atmosphere and throwing them behind her.

Some critics have held that *The Charwoman's Daughter* lacks a dimension of social realism, not to mention social protest; that the idyllic tone and the comic idiom soften out of significance the crude social realities—which are clearly present on every page. There is some truth in the charge. Leaving down the book the reader can be left only with an aura of romance and wonder, the sense of an enchanted, sunlit city. But it is equally true that in the process of reading the novel the entire thrust of its plot depends on the most precise sense of Dublin's social inequalities and of the author's conviction, expressed in Chapter 24, 'that there is only one grave and debasing vice in the world, and that is poverty'. The mother's anger in the passage quoted hinges on that central proposition, as does her repeated admonition to Mary, 'Never be a servant in your heart.' It could be argued that the book's success derives from the fact that these convictions are not stated but embodied; and that they are aesthetically distanced by the devices of humour and parody through which the action is filtered. The confrontation of the policeman and the charwoman gains an exquisite dimension of irony when we become aware that the former is preening himself in an old-fashioned posture of hierarchy: he is for the moment posing as the rich squire questioning his domestic servant about the age and character of her attractive daughter. It is the clownish pretension of his patronage that makes the mother's recoil so splendidly comic. And the incident, related to us at this remove, prepares us for the far more serious confrontation in the tenement, in Chapter 30, where the intrigue is brought to light and painfully resolved by mother, daughter and suitor.

The effectiveness of this proposal scene—which in its formality and convention reminds us of so many similar scenes in traditional English fiction, notably in Jane Austen—derives in great measure from its structural placing in the novel. It represents the momentous encroachment of the public action upon the private and domestic. The drama is made tense by the smallness of the room and the huge incongruity of the policeman. His towering authority is cowed and diminished by the surroundings, and by the two silent women. He does not know that everything he says is agonisingly new to the mother, and the current of feeling between the three gives a dimension of painful irony to his discourse. The reader is aware of his mission being doomed, but this knowledge is shared only with Mary. Against this background his proposal, backed by all the conventional arguments of mutual attraction, financial stability, steadiness of personal character, falls like meaningless dead weight through the atmosphere. For the first time in the novel he appears not as a caricature but as a fully articulated character in the process of final defeat; for the first time he makes a genuine demand on the reader's sympathy. But within the novel's economy he is now relevant only as an agent through whom the lesion between mother and daughter is exposed and the process of Mary's maturation is finally achieved and demonstrated.

The process of growth is two-fold. Mary's advance to womanhood necessarily involves a like process in the charwoman. The world of makebelieve is shattered and their relationship must now proceed in the light of reality. This process is managed by Stephens with less elaboration than the earlier stages of the drama; the reconciliation of mother and daughter is told rather than demonstrated :

> Mrs Makebelieve saw seventeen years' apprenticeship to maternity cancelled automatically without an explanation or a courtesy, and for a little time her world was in ruins, the ashes of existence powdered her hair and her forehead. Then she discovered that the debris was valuable in known currency; the dust was golden : her love remained to her undisturbed and unlikely to be disturbed by whatever event. And she discovered that parentage is neither a game nor a privilege, but a duty !

The Dickensian briskness of these summary resolutions—we must not forget that it was a serial novel—does not seriously impair the book's shape or balance. The main action ends and the fairy-tale *dénouement* provides a satisfactory conclusion. Uncle Patrick's will rescues mother and daughter not merely from poverty but from the necessity of further recrimination. The young clerk with his dreams of a socialist Utopia and a free Ireland furnishes Mary with a more congruous, if no less transient, suitor. The morphology of the fairy tale closes round the drama of sexual and spiritual growth, of social unhappiness, of mother-love and domestic tension. The light of 'romance' plays back over the novel's action softening the angles of its realism, its satire and its irony.

The Early Poetry

The Problem of Influence

For most of his writing career Stephens alternated between prose and verse, and in both directions his tendency was experimental. But while his experiments in fiction present a coherent pattern, a sense of ground steadily gained and intelligently consolidated, his poetic experiments appear by contrast random and capricious, a series of advances, swerves, hesitations and retreats. He develops no consistent attitude to language or technique, nor does he develop, except in the final volumes, a central core of thematic concern. At every stage of his development he is surprisingly open to new influences: his current reading in poetry at any stage of his career could almost be deduced from his own poetic practice. *Insurrections*, published in 1909, is a less derivative book than *The Hill of Vision* which came out three years later. Both of them are more original than his 1915 volume, *Songs from the Clay*, which is more a valley of Georgian echoes than an individual poet's verse. On the other hand *Reincarnations* (1918), by far his best single volume, has more in common with *Insurrections* than with anything written in between, notably its concrete and colloquial idiom, its satire, its comic energy. It might be argued that his last two mystical volumes, *Strict Joy* (1931) and *Kings and the Moon* (1938)[1] exhibit a thematic unity of concern but it would have to be conceded that they offer no corresponding sophistication of language, form or technique, and that the voice of Stephens is too often drowned out by the voices of Shakespeare, Blake, Emerson and Emily Dickinson.

Though he was almost thirty when it appeared in 1909, *Insurrections* has the verve and freshness, together with the stridency and unevenness, of a young man's first work. The poet's insurgency is social, religious and poetic. There is a recurrent note of rebellion against society whether voiced directly by the writer himself as in 'Fifty Pounds a Year and a Pension', or dramatised through the voices of his created personae. In counterpoint with the social protest there is a persistent, various and often ambiguous complaint lodged with God for his role in the sorry scheme of things. The poetic insurgency is implicit: the language seems often rudely indecorous for its time and place—'Let them drain / Their porter-pots and snuffle'—so that George Moore, in his *Vale*, could find in the young poet's work 'little more than harsh versification, and crude courage in the choice of subjects'.

Seen against the background of Irish and English poetry of the time the choice of subjects is certainly remarkable—a girl dancing for a drunken audience in a pub, a woman telling her red-haired husband that he will never possess her, a drunken visionary confiding to his cronies that he has seen God the Father, a copying clerk cursing god and fate, an old man climbing a cliff with a rope to hang himself, Ould Snarly Gob by the fire vowing impotent vengeance on his contemporaries, a rapacious lover chasing a girl through the fields, a tramp swearing at the discomfort of life, a battered old jarvey taking a passenger to the Four Courts, an aged whore trailing a potential customer through the city's slums.[2] The fact that the dramatic lyric, with its possibility of different voices, predominates is not in itself new; it has been a favoured form of Yeats, Campbell and Colum; but their imagined personae have been mostly idealised country people, peasants, fishermen, parish priests, fiddlers, mountainy singers, tinkers, poor scholars. The city context and decor is new. Yeats had not yet entered on his dialogue with the 'unmannerly town' or undergone his 'baptism of the gutter'. Nor had there been any significant poetry of the city in the older Irish tradition. English poetry—if we exclude a few mannered stanzas from Wilde and Dowson—is still mainly bucolic, waiting, as it were, for Prufrock. *Insurrections* is furthermore free from the self-conscious 'Irishness' that had held sway in Irish literature for more than a century. There are no fairy hosts, no Celtic heroes or Celtic

Twilights. This is not to say that the question of influence does
not arise. With few writers does it arise in such varied and complex manifestation.

In one of his many discussions of poetic influence Harold
Bloom quotes Borges's famous remark that 'every writer *creates
his own precursors*', and goes on to identify the process as an
'anxiety principle' which forces the poet to look back nervously
at the work of certain predecessors in relation to his own : 'Have
they left him room enough, or has their priority cost him his art?
More crucially, where did they go wrong, so as to make it possible
for him to go right? In this revisionary sense, in which the poet
creates his own precursors by necessarily misinterpreting them,
poetic influence forms and malforms new poets, and aids their
art at the cost of increasing, finally, their already acute sense of
isolation.'[3] The phenomenon upon which Bloom insists is primarily a Romantic one which finds obvious expression in Blake's
Milton or in Yeats's response to Shelley. But the conflict seems
rarely to arise in the case of minor poets, and that is perhaps the
factor that makes them minor. By and large they seem content
to beg, borrow or steal from their elders when they are young,
and when they find their individual voices they express themselves more often in a spirit of unconscious liberation rather than
of conscious triumph.

Stephens's influences came to him sporadically and variously
and he seems to have had no coherent policy for dealing with
them except one of spontaneous and uncritical hospitality. He is
positively gleeful in his sense of debt to Spenser, Milton, Blake,
Wordsworth, Browning, AE, Ralph Hodgson and so many others.
When he came to assemble his *Collected Poems* of 1926 he had
attained to enough self-criticism to exclude from it much that
had been too blatantly derivative, but at no time do we find him
resentful of its several sources. He remained proud of the incident
which, he claimed, set him writing in the first place. He once
bought two books, one by Blake and one by Browning, and took
them home to bed : 'I started reading in bed and my mind said
to me "You can do that," and that night I wrote twenty-five
poems.'[4] And it was without guilt that he endorsed Fuseli's
famous remark on Blake that he was 'good to steal from'. Certainly it would be difficult to discuss his first volume without
reference to Blake and Browning, just as it would be perverse to

discuss his second without considering the cluster of new writers who came quickly and often banefully to his attention in the three years that separated the two publications. There is, fortunately, to hand his own account of his reading before and during this period of rapid change and development.

In 1913 Ernest Boyd, who was later to be the historian of the Irish Literary Revival, wrote to him in Paris on the subject of his 'influences' and received this reply: 'As to your questions—What Irish writer influenced me most? None of 'em singly, but I did soak myself to the scalp & beyond in the older Irish writers. The newer school, Russell, Yeats, Colum, O'Grady, etc. were entirely unknown to me when I began to write.'[5] This account of his 'influences' is confirmed by any careful reading of his first two volumes. There is no echo of the 'newer' school in *Insurrections* while in *The Hill of Vision* their influence, especially that of Russell, is clearly traceable.

Browning and the Dramatic Lyric

Stephens's debt to Browning is especially evident in the dramatic lyrics and monologues. Browning's sense of character and idiosyncrasy, the abrupt vigour of his language, his sense of dramatic situation, and his irreverent scorn of organised religion presented him as an exemplar to be followed rather than a precursor to be overcome. The influence was entirely wholesome because Stephens, while adopting Browning's method—scenario with speaking persona, audience and situation—insisted on applying it to his own very different social and cultural milieu, thereby achieving a successful mating of content and form while avoiding mere sedulous imitation.

'The Dancer' with which the book opens exhibits both the virtues and the defects of the poet's early dramatic manner. The dancer is his first type for trapped humanity, oppressed by an uncaring and exploitative society and further oppressed, as appears in the second and third stanzas, by an indifferent deity. The scenario is elaborate to the point of melodrama: not only is the dancer repelled by the audience—'Those booted hogs and lechers!'—but her beloved lies dead at home. The vehemence and stridency of the language is characteristic of the more dramatic pieces in the book:

I will not dance!
I say I will not dance.
Your audience! Pah! Let them go home again,
Sleek, ugly pigs! Am I to hop and prance
As long as they will pay!
And posture for their eyes! And lay
My womanhood before them! Let them drain
Their porter-pots and snuffle—I'll not stay!

Given its excess of shrillness and melodrama the verse is not without accomplishment. The woman is real, visually palpable, stamping her foot to those staccato rhythms, no less a dancer because she has ceased to dance. The pattern of rhyme and metre is easily overlooked; the verse seems on first sight so random and unstructured. But it is consistently sustained through the three stanzas, responding with tact and sympathy to varying intensity of tone and mood. The concreteness and colloquialism of the diction, the genuine sense of a human voice speaking is equally remarkable considering the current literary climate. These are the technical considerations.

More importantly the poem evinces passionate concern with a central area of contemporary human anxiety and one in which the poet's sympathies are closely engaged. He is perplexed and angry with the way in which society, under an allegedly benign god, has distributed its gifts and privileges. In the midst of his city he is moved, as Eliot is soon to be, by

The notion of some infinitely gentle
Infinitely suffering thing.[6]

He lacks so far the urbanity to draw his theme to precise or delicate definition. For the moment he is groping for a poetic form that will at least bring it into visible focus. His method is the interrogation of chosen witnesses in a court that consists of the suffering individual, the uncaring society, the indifferent deity:

O, God! You tramp
Upon me, too; and twine
More sorrows round me than are mine
With holy unconcern.... Don't bar my way
I'm going to my dead.... Ah, stamping swine.

In 'Where the Demons Grin' the narrator watches while an old man climbs to a cliff-top muttering bitterly to himself about divine injustice, his dead wife, and 'hungry children craving bread'. He is a terminal case in Stephens's landscape of social and religious hopelessness :

> He held a rope; and as he trod,
> Pressing against the furious wind,
> He muttered low and sneered at God
> And said He sure was deaf or blind,
> Or lazing on the sod.

A 'demon up from hell' jabbers as the old man falls to his death. The scenario is even more extravagantly factitious than in 'The Dancer'. The facility of the rhymes betrays a general slackness of language. Stephens never quite overcomes his weakness for hackneyed and exhausted prosody. To the end of his writing career he remains unembarrassed by the conjunction of 'wind' and 'blind', 'God' and 'sod'. Such indifference would be insignificant in a poet of less capacity or promise. It is when we see his language working at full stretch that we realise how little it would have taken—competent criticism, study of the right contemporaries, appreciation of Eliot or Pound whom he actively rejected[7]—to give coherence and direction to his development. His picture of the jarvey, another version of his oppressed individual, is perhaps the most vivid of his human sketches in this first collection :

> The driver rubbed his nettly chin
> With a huge loose forefinger, crooked and black;
> And his wobbly violet lips sucked in,
> And puffed out again and hung down slack :
> A black fang shone through his lop-sided smile,
> In his little pouched eye flickered years of guile.[8]

The poem is sympathetic; it ends with a prayer for both horse and driver. But the physical portraiture is precise and uncompromising. The language is vital and adequate. In the verbal force of the adjectives and the kinetic precision of the verbs the slack, plaintive mobility of the old man's face comes to life. The emotional sympathy that declares itself, perhaps damagingly, in the final stanza is kept at arm's length here by the palpable ugliness of the 'black fang' and the watchful 'pouched eye'. But this kind of success cannot be found with any consistency in the pages of *Insurrections*. And it is one of his misfortunes as a writer that he did not persist with and develop his initial, and apparently instinctive, skill with spoken language; especially as this was what the more important poets of his time were striving to recover. Instead he digressed into 'mysticism' on the one hand and Georgian pastoralism on the other in the years immediately ahead.

The dramatic method of the persona, oddly akin to Yeats's 'phantasmagoria',[9] seems to have been necessary for Stephens when grappling with his social and spiritual perplexities. In his one attempt to confront these issues in direct autobiographical poetry, in 'Fifty Pounds a Year and a Pension' (C.P., p. 209) he tries another version of the triadic structure—the individual, society, the deity—and achieves a peculiarly graceless result :

> But I'll sit and work my utmost and not budge;
> Tho' a grudge
> Is ever growing in the bosom of a clod
> 'Gainst a God
> Who condemned him in his lifetime to grow fit
> For the pit.

He is perhaps too close to the action to sustain his role in the triangle of forces.

Before moving on from this initial and revealing area of Stephens's early poetry it will be helpful to look at one poem, this time from his second volume, in which he achieves a notable success with the dramatic lyric and the theme of cosmic injustice :

'Bessie Bobtail' achieves a blend of accuracy, compassion and dramatic force together with a surefooted economy of detail that we have not yet seen. The first stanza presents the mad old woman muttering her so far inaudible complaint :

> She stumped along, and wagged her pate
> And said a thing was desperate.

The offbeat rhyme and the conversational ellipsis mark an advance in economy and tautness in the poet's technique. The second stanza moves through a series of deft pictorial touches and recapitulations during which the old woman's words are still withheld. In the last stanza he quietly inserts himself, as listener, into the picture, and the focus sharpens :

> I walked behind her for a while,
> And watched the people nudge and smile :
> But even as she went, she said,
> As left and right she swung her head,
> 'Oh, God he knows! Ah, God he knows!'
> And, surely God Almighty knows.[10]

The poem's success is due to its simplicity and its reticence. Stephens has learned not to insist too much, to keep the fierceness of his personal voice out of the drama, to permit the occasion to speak for itself. The effect is strengthened by the rhythmic movement, its repetitions, its trudging sense of a sideward as well as an onward motion, its suggestion of the old woman's halting progress, the stubbornness of her will, the futility, if not the ultimate exhaustion of her hope.

Blake and the Poetry of Vision

> The first night that I read Blake I wrote fifteen poems, and I kept like that for a year. It was as though I had found a father and a mother and a fortune. A phrase from him could set me drunk, and if I did not always understand what he was saying, understand that is in terms of logic, I knew what he was saying by the sense he wakened in me, by the emotion which was like a bridge thrown between the dead man and the living.[11]

The role of Blake as both poetic exemplar and moral teacher is chiefly evident in those 'vision' poems in which God, Satan and the angels appear with speaking parts in the dramatic scenario. As with Browning there appears to be no effort to resist or struggle with the English poet's influence. What originality the poems achieve comes, ironically, not from conflict but from assent.

The Protestantism which Stephens had been shedding in these early creative years is gradually replaced by Blake's more life-affirming system, so that the young poet seems content to write a series of glosses on the great Romantic's lyrical and visionary utterances. Stephens's sense of the injustices everywhere visible in his own city makes Blake's commentaries on London something like texts in a gospel to be expanded and annotated. Blake's rejec-

B

tion of the traditional christian god coincides with Stephens's own distrust of his inherited christianity. Blake's apotheosis of the imagination, his doctrine of god within man, his insistence on the primacy of passion over reason proved valuable to Stephens who was already in rebellion against the restrictive morality of his institutional upbringing. Above all Blake's example enabled Stephens to get on top of things, to dominate the world outside him by the use of poetic imagination. His first vision poem, which appeared in *Insurrections* and is entitled 'What Tomas an Buile Said in a Pub'[12] reveals the nature of the influence.

The vision is clearly Blakean—it could be a verbal impression of the Creator in Blake's Plate showing the morning stars singing together at creation. That he should wish to mediate the vision through the persona of Mad Tomas may betoken an unwillingness on Stephens's part to discard the dramatic monologue, or on the other hand to commit himself fully, as yet, to a direct responsibility for the poem's theological implications:

> His beard swung on a wind far out of sight
> Behind the world's curve, and there was light
> Most fearful from His forehead, and he sighed,
> 'That star went always wrong, and from the start
> I was dissatisfied.'

The star in question is that mentioned by Tess of the d'Urbervilles before the night mail strikes her cart, our earth, god's refractory planet where a pattern of injustice, suffering and oppression endures and persists. The deity visualised is a combination of Blake's Nobodaddy and Urizen, the 'Father of Jealousy'. But Stephens consistently calls him 'God the Father' and in this respect appropriates him for the drama of his own moral debate. Here the creator is about to strike out the planet in despair, raising a 'dreadful hand over the spinning earth' when Tomas intervenes:

> . . . then I said 'Stay,
> You must not strike it, God; I'm in the way:
> And I will never move from where I stand.'
> He said 'Dear Child, I feared that you were dead.'
> And stayed his hand.

This is the first, and one of the mildest, of Stephens's attempts

to draw this Old Testament god out of his obscurity in the clouds
so as to question his present relationship with his universe and to
make him answerable in the imaginative debate that Stephens
is conducting on the condition of the world, moral, social,
theological. God the Father is unhappy with the world. He still
has power to annihilate it; it is not clear whether he can mend
it. The only check on his desire to have done with the unhappy
enterprise is a residual compassion for the creatures who may still
want to shoulder the burden of existence. For the moment Mad
Tomas has been the world's saviour. By repeatedly placing god in
this position of impotent distress and divine remoteness Stephens
challenges the theology which still gives its sanction to an unjust
social order in the world. Bessie Bobtail has insisted that 'surely
God Almighty knows', to which Stephens now provides the
answer: yes, he knows, he may even care, but he is powerless to
set things right.

In 'What the Devil Said' (C.P., p. 132) the same 'God the
Father, Good', hears a feeble cry coming to him from the distance
and sends his gaze down through the universe to find its source.
It passes the 'whistling stars, bright as a wizard's day', the 'ice-
capped pole', the sea that 'swung round the world in surgent
energy':

> But these He passed, with eyes intently wide,
> Till, closer still, the mountains he espied
> Squatting tremendous on the broad-backed Earth,
> Each nursing twenty rivers at a birth!
> And then, minutely, sought He for the cry
> Had climbed the slant of space so hugely high.

The journey of the divine vision through the universe is sharply
monitored in the increasing particularity of the verbs; the forward pressure exercised by 'intently' is reinforced by 'minutely';
the coldness of the universe and the isolation of creator from
creature are given vivid and simultaneous expression. The gran-
diose and chilling visions of the evolutionists are ironically
counterpointed against the blander consolations of 'natural
theology'. The heavens do and they don't 'declare the glory of
God'. But in the poem's conclusion they seem to have little
function in the commonwealth of his creatures:

He found it in a ditch outside a town :
A tattered hungry woman, crouching down
By a dead babe— So there was naught to do,
For what is done is done ! And sad He drew
Back to His Heaven of ivory and gold :
And, as He sat, all suddenly there rolled,
From where the woman wept upon the sod,
Satan's deep voice—'O thou unhappy God !'

Though Stephens's god has a good deal in common with Blake's Nobodaddy he is distinct from him in one important respect. Blake's deity delights in 'hanging and drawing and quartering/ Every bit as well as war and slaughtering'.[13] Stephens's god, in the face of human suffering, is impotent and appalled. His creation has wandered beyond his control. He can say with Blake's Urizen, 'Lo, I am God, the terrible destroyer, and not the Saviour,' but he is past relishing such punitive dominion. A residue of guilty compassion deters him from annihilating the world, but it is not sufficient to attract the love of his creatures. In as far as he exists at all for Stephens he is doomed to inhabit his own created 'vacancies of Heaven', a sort of loveless interstellar limbo. Thus the long and unsuccessful poem, 'The Lonely God',[14] with which *The Hill of Vision* ends, shows him finally seeking the comradeship of Eve and Adam whom he has banished from Eden. And in a shorter but more effective poem, 'In the Cool of the Evening' (C.P., p. 131) he presents God's dilemma from the human perspective. Eve in the garden, hearing God approach, imagines that he is coming to inflict further punishment. She urges Adam to crouch with her out of sight :

O that it were night !
He may not come . . . What ? listen, listen, now
He's here ! lie closer . . . *Adam, where art thou?*

Adam has slunk away. It is the Fall in microcosm and may well be Stephens's deliberate gloss on Blake's 'Night the First' where the human faculties separate in chaos and disharmony dramatising man's collapse into the unhappy world of Ulro. If read in conjunction with 'The Lonely God' the poem reveals an added irony and pathos : in the former, God had come to his creatures not in wrath but in need. By mistrusting his intentions Eve reveals a universe of relentless cross-purposes.

Satan's role in the drama is no less ironical. In 'What the Devil Said' he is capable of compassion both for creatures and for creator. Yet he too seems impotent. In 'The Fullness of Time' (C.P., p. 234) he occupies a position as remote and dejected as that of his heavenly antagonist :

> On a rusty iron throne
> Past the furthest star of space
> I saw Satan sit alone,
> Old and haggard was his face;
> For his work was done, and he
> Rested in eternity.

The poem goes on to narrate his reconciliation with the hosts of heaven and his apotheosis as they place him beside 'One who had been crucified'. Stephens obviously looks forward to a time when the distinctions between good and evil, god and devil, will be resolved. One is tempted to seek in this handful of visionary poems a small-scale sequence or pattern moving, on the Blakean parallel, from creation to apocalypse. This would tend to exaggerate their coherence and distort their deeper significance. Such significance relates to the question of Stephens's actual belief in god, devil, heaven and hell. Here the example of Blake is useful both as comparison and contrast.

Blake believed in God, Father, Son and Holy Ghost, though he tended to concentrate on Jesus, the 'Divine Humanity'. Therefore when Blake writes of that distortion of the Father, Nobodaddy, he is not mocking God. He is deriding a figure that exists only as an obscene figment of a deformed theological imagination, a bloodthirsty idol created by official religion for the enslavement of man. Stephens's God the Father is of roughly the same order but with this difference, that Stephens does not appear to believe in the deity of which his divine persona is a distortion. While his treatment of God and Satan is not as derisory as that employed by Blake towards Nobodaddy, it is still parodic. They are persistently imaged as exhausted icons of traditional religion and morality sponsoring a system of values that can no longer claim the allegiance of contemporary man. By presenting them as he does, by giving them their traditional roles and attitudes, and by testing them against his own concepts of humane morality, he contrives to dislodge them progressively from their place among his own inherited values. The fact that neither God nor Satan can sustain his expected role is a symptom of their obsolescence. Our response to their dilemmas as presented by the poet is not ultimately to sympathise with them but to discard and forget them. They have no longer a role to play. Thus Satan's last flicker of energy occurs in a poem entitled 'The Nodding Stars'[15] published three years after *The Hill of Vision*, where the fallen Lucifer tiredly rebukes the stars for asking him to persist in his warfare with heaven :

> If ye mean revolt ! If ye
> Raise the standard ! Do not seek
> Help or heartening from me.
> I am powerless, am weak,
>
> Am clipped of wing ! The crown of old
> Would not fit me now ! My rage
> Is as dreadful as the scold
> Of a linnet in a cage !
>
> O, my dears ! I'm nodding too !
> Hard as ever I can try !
> Up, and up, and up, to you,
> Where you nod upon the sky !

What we are witnessing here, albeit through a haze of whimsy, is the death of Satan, and of god, the angels, the devils, their works and their pomps, in the poet's imagination. They have been, with whatever degree of deliberation, parodied out of existence. Once this is recognised, the finely irreverent and Byronic 'Mac Dhoul'[16] becomes sharply significant. This Diony-siac ruffian has somehow been transported to the heavenly court

> With two weeks' whisker blackening lug to lug,
> With tattered breeks and only half a shirt !

From this vantage point he presents his mocking description of the divine milieu :

> To see them at their capers;
> That serious, solemn-footed, weighty crowd
> Of angels—or, say, resurrected drapers !

As God approaches, the hero leaps mischievously on to the empty throne where he sits 'Squirming with laughter' only to be flicked by the creator back to earth. The journey is familiar :

> ... And then adown I sped
> Scraping old moons and twisting heels and head,[17]
> A chuckle in the void, till ... here I stand
> As naked as a brick,
> I'll sing the Peeler and the Goat in half a tick.

Mac Dhoul means 'son of the devil'. The 'Peeler and the Goat' is a ballad about a policeman who attempts to arrest a goat for being drunk and disorderly. Stephens is the goat, God the celestial policeman. From here on they are to go their separate ways.

These two early volumes of poetry are best seen as lyrical excogitation and debate. In the course of them Stephens works his way clear of what has now become for him a dead theology, has tamed the minatory agents of traditional religion, clipped the wings of the more threatening angels. He has used his creative imagination to secure for himself a world-view that is credible, workable and liberating. In so far as he continues to write of the everyday world it is to be free from the strictures of an oppressive social morality sanctioned by a punitive and inexplicable deity. Because his imagination is the agency that has set him free it follows that the same agency can henceforth insist on dominating experience. He has Blake to thank for much of this, and the opening poem to *The Hill of Vision* can now be seen in terms of Blake's theory of imaginative perception :[18]

> Everything that I can spy
> Through the circle of my eye,
> Everything that I can see
> Has been woven out of me.
> I have sown the stars; I threw
> Clouds of morn and noon and eve
> In the deeps and steeps of blue;
> And each thing that I perceive,
> Sun and sea and mountain high,
> Are made and moulded by my eye :
> Closing it, I do but find
> Darkness, and a little wind.[19]

The poem plainly asserts the autonomy of the imagination, the dominance of the perceiving and creating mind over the material world. It throws valuable light forward on the writer's imaginative activity in creating the world of the prose fantasies, and it illumines the poetic activity that went into the drama of God, Satan and man in the poems of vision.

The poet's final gesture in his cosmic debate occurs in a poem entitled 'The Tramp's Dream', which appears in his 1915 volume, *Songs from the Clay*. He excludes it from his collected edition, probably because it was written at a time when its theme was no longer a live question in the writer's mind. It is almost self-parody. The tramp sees a vision of the last judgment in which the 'blind and battered and the lewd and lame' wait for the appearance of god in his role of judge:

> And as He walked in fire
> Those million, million muzzles lifted higher,
> Stared at Him, grinned in fury, toned a yelp,
> A vast malignant query, 'Did you help?'

Clearly the poet's more serious emotions are no longer engaged. He has, by then, turned to a different system of belief for which the iconography of traditional christianity is no longer relevant—the transcendentalism of AE and the Theosophists.

AE and Mysticism

To appreciate this change it is necessary to distinguish between Stephens's 'visionary' and his 'mystical' poems. Northrop Frye has usefully discriminated between these two terms in dealing with the poetry of Blake. For him Blake is not a 'mystic' in the orthodox sense of the term, because strict mysticism 'is a form of spiritual communion with God which is by its nature incommunicable to anyone else, and which soars beyond faith into direct apprehension'. Blake, he insists, is a 'visionary', one who 'creates, or dwells in, a higher spiritual world in which the objects of perception in this one have become transfigured and charged with a new intensity of symbolism'.[20] In this sense the poetry of Stephens which has so far been considered, inasmuch as it aspires to either condition, is visionary, and has been thus described. It has involved a conception of god which has been all too communicable, so much so that it has been possible to see it as parodic and dismissive.

Already, however, the religion—if one can call it that—which is being elided is also being replaced, as early as *The Hill of Vision*, with an outlook that might properly be called 'mystical'. A letter to Stephen MacKenna towards the end of 1914 provides a valuable insight to his progress in both theological and poetic belief :

> I still think that in the Lonely God there are some good verses, and that the subject (as a mere painting or landscape, or canvas) was vast enough to satisfy the craving for "vastness" which then (& now) was an ever-present desire with me. I recollect that A.E., in criticising this poem complained that he preferred my tinker drunk to my God sober. In truth while I have a continuous feeling of and for God, I had another as continuous feeling of and for woman : and (the whole ill is here) I mixed the unmixables. The God of that poem is too anthropomorphic even for poetry. But in those days I did not expect nor suspect an Absolute, & was willing to credit deity with my own desires, and very generously to confer these on Him. Well, I suppose I am the only poet that ever married God the Father. It was well meant.[21]

The self-deprecation arises from the fact that he had represented god as needing, in his aloneness, the comfort of Eve. The artist in him, tempered in the crucible of three works of fiction, recognises the implausibility of that theme for a work of narrative poetry. The religious thinker in him, more significantly, has come to a radically different view of the god-head. Under the influence of AE and the theosophical exegetes he has come to a mystical apprehension of god who now appears as 'the Absolute'. It was a view which would in time enable him, as thinker, to repudiate Blake's visionary account of the world, and of the artist's ministry in it. Thus in a B.B.C. broadcast on Blake in 1945, he had so detached himself from Blake's doctrines as to speak of him in these terms :

> He states outright and downright that God's own self, the Unutterable Transcendency, is with him in the day and in the night, and does not merely inspire his song, but actually and

audibly and verbally dictates it to him in South Molton Street, London, W.C.

Speaking as a versifier myself, I prefer the poetic 'form' of Spenser or Donne or Keats to the poetic 'form' of the Prophetic dictation.[22]

The phrase 'Unutterable Transcendency' reveals Stephens's new —and what is to be his final—concept of the deity. And this concept of divinity has already begun to invest his thought while he is still writing his 'visionary' poetry in *The Hill of Vision*. The turning point is a poem entitled 'The Breath of Life' (C.P., p. 225) which, though written at the same period, is not located among the visionary poems in his collected edition. It is worth considering in full.

It is a 'mystical' poem, a poem about the 'Unutterable Transcendent' in which the poet attempts to communicate the incommunicable. It begins in the idiom of his dramatic lyrics: the poet represents himself as listening to an abstract ethical discussion on the nature of good and evil:

> And while they talked and talked, and while they sat
> Changing their base minds into baser coin;
> And telling—they! how truth and beauty join,
> And how a certain this was good, but that
> Was baser than the viper or the toad,
> Or the blind beggar glaring down the road.

It proceeds by telling how the listener 'turned from them in fury', left the company, and was rewarded by contact with the divine principle:

> The Breath that is the very Breath of Life
> Throbbed close to me! I heard the pulses beat,
> That lift the universes into heat!
> The slow withdrawal, and the deeper strife
> Of His wide respiration—like a sea
> It ebbed and flooded through immensity.

The poem is breathless, ecstatic, devotional and in its way persuasive and impressive. Its focus is the deity of AE's mystical belief, a spiritual force unknowable except in its effects on the individual soul, explicable only in metaphors of silence, reverence, the caress of mysterious indescribable love:

The silence clung about me like a gift!
The tender night-time folded me around
Protectingly! And in a peace profound,
The clouds drooped slowly backwards, drift on drift
Into the darkness;

The force of the mystical experience is to render irrelevant the
ethical discussion which is the poem's point of departure. In the
presence of the great breath the poet finds a sense of 'boundless
gratitude for boundless love'. His new god is the antithesis of the
biblical caricature of the early dramatic lyrics. The crisis of
human suffering and earthly injustice which had been the occasion of these early poems is now miraculously abolished:

Rejoicing in the viper and the toad;
And the blind beggar glaring down the road
And they, who talk and talk and never stop,
Equally quickening!

In the new-found scheme of things, one can only assume, both
the ethical discussion with which the poem opened and the incidental misery of the blind beggar are resolved in a universal love.
The great breath harmonises a universe of different karmic
planes of which the earth, with its miseries and aberrations, is
only one. This 'mystical' sense of the numinous is, again, radically
distinct from Blake's concept of god in man. Stephens's deity is
in no sense 'anthropomorphic', is so transcendent as to be un-
reachable in terms of human knowledge or indeed of poetic
imagination. It is in the strict terms of Stephens's own language
—which is that of AE and Blavatsky—'Unutterable Transcendency'. Poetry can only describe it by its effect on the soul in
ecstasy, and this effect can be rendered only by incorrigibly
vague and approximate metaphor. In the light of a poem such
as this, a poem like 'The Tramp's Dream', already glanced at,
can only be seen as a parody of religious beliefs now obsolete
in the poet's consciousness. From this point forward Stephens
gives increasingly less attention in his poetry to questions of social
injustice and divine indifference. He becomes more and more
absorbed in mystical doctrine. It does not immediately appear as
a major theme in his poetry for reasons that will become evident.
But when it does, in the twenties, it dominates his poetry to the
end.

Male and Female

We have already seen in *The Charwoman's Daughter* a version of the male-female relationship in the struggle between Mary and the Policeman. This theme, which persists through the body of Stephens's fiction, is central to his early poetry. His view of man and woman and the drama of their encounter derives in part from Blake, in part from theosophical doctrine, but is ultimately peculiar to Stephens himself. The attraction and opposition of man and woman, their mutual capacity for conquest and surrender, their eternal vacillation between love and enmity, constitute his most enduring theme in both the poetry and the fiction. It is the basic preoccupation of the novels and short stories, the subject of his most memorable epigrams and the fulcrum of his meditations on human existence. In a poem from his first volume, 'The Red-Haired Man's Wife' (C.P., p. 73), it finds early and forceful expression. The speaker in this extended dramatic monologue takes up an attitude similar to that of the 'Dancer' but is more archetypal in her tone, more measured and mannered in her assertion:

> I have taken a vow!
> And you were my friend
> But yesterday—Now
> All that's at an end;
> And you are my husband, and claim me, and I must
> depend.

The monologue is internal: the lover, turned husband, is unaware of the change that is taking place and his uncomprehending presence in the scenario is essential to the irony of the poem's process:

> Yesterday I was free!
> Now you, as I stand,
> Walk over to me
> And take hold of my hand;
> You look at my lips! Your eyes are too bold, your smile
> is too bland!

He has made the first false move, he has presumed too much in his readiness to take what she, had it been properly sought, had

been ready to surrender. He has presumed in seizing to himself
the perilous authority of the contract; he has thrown the dead
weight of the social law against the primal and mysterious female
principle; in this sense he has offended against the mysteries:

> My old name is lost;
> My distinction of race!
> Now the line has been crossed,
> Must I step to your pace?
> Must I walk as you list, and obey and smile up in your
> face?

The line has been crossed in two senses: her lineage has been
cancelled with her name; her husband has crossed the line of
their separateness, instead of meeting her there. The last two
lines suggest, in a dramatic way, the pattern of social convention
and appearance he now expects her to adopt. Consequently the
woman's allegiance is to her separateness, the female principle.
The rhetoric of their relationship is to be war instead of love; on
her side defiance instead of submission. The rhetoric of the
poem, which is less a matter of argument than of cumulative
assertion, is to define the tension which the husband's first disastrous presumption has imposed:

> Oh, if kneeling were right,
> I should kneel nor be sad!
> And abase in your sight
> All the pride that I had!
> I should come to you, hold to you, call to you, glad.

Thrown back on her female separateness she determines to culti-
vate ancient patterns of conflict as the ground on which to con-
duct the dialogue of psychic warfare: 'I am woman, and glory,
and beauty; I mystery, terror and doubt!' The Christian ideal
of marriage proposes a union of flesh and spirit; Stephens is suggesting an older and less comforting reality of primal, and perhaps ineradicable opposition:

> I am separate still!
> I am I and not you!
> And my mind and my will,
> As in secret they grew,

Still are secret; unreached, and untouched, and not subject to you.

Nora Crionna, whose name suggests ironically that she is wise
in her generation,[23] sins against this secret separateness of man
and woman by too much solicitude : she tries

To peep behind his frowning eye
With little query, little pry
And make him, if a woman can,
Happier than any man.

She has tried to trivialise the mystery, to domesticate the myth,
and she is punished with suitable severity :

—Yesterday he gripped her tight
And cut her throat. And serve her right !

Whether expressed in terms of archetypal dialogue or black
comedy this war of the sexes persists as a serious theme through
the bulk of Stephens's creative thought. And as it will present
itself in a wide variety of manifestations in the prose fantasy it
is as well to anticipate briefly his most direct statement on the
subject in his novel, *The Demi-Gods*. Here is his authorial com-
mentary on the state of his heroine, Mary MacCann, at an important moment of her development :

Mary, who could make women do anything for her, was
entirely interested in making men bow to her will, and because
almost against her expectation, they did bow, she loved them,
and could not sacrifice herself too much to their comfort and
even their caprice. It was the mother-spirit in her which,
observing the obedience of her children, is forced in very
gratitude to become their slave; for, beyond all things, a
woman desires power, and, beyond all things she is unable to
use it when she gets it. If this power be given to her grudgingly
she will exercise it mercilessly; if it is given kindly, then she
is bound by her nature to renounce authority, and to live
happy ever after, but it must be given to her.[24]

The happiness of the sexes on earth in this, as in all of
Stephens's pronouncements on the subject, requires spectacular
resources of generosity, humility and tact on both sides. It is not

therefore surprising that we find few examples of harmonious marriage in his poetry or fiction. The opposing principles of the male and the female exercise themselves in a manner similar to Blake's vision of earthly marriage as dramatised, for instance, in his *Jerusalem*, Plate 69 :

> Then all the Males conjoined into One Male & every one
> Became a ravening eating Cancer growing in the Female,
> ....
> That they might be born in contentions of Chastity & in
> Deadly Hate between Leah & Rachel, Daughters of Deceit &
> Fraud
> Bearing the Images of various Species of Contention
> And Jealousy & Abhorrence & Revenge & deadly Murder,
> Till they refuse liberty to the Male, & not like Beulah
> Where every Female delights to give her maiden to her
> husband :
> The Female searches sea & land for gratifications to the
> Male Genius, who in return clothes her in gems & gold
> And feeds her with the food of Eden;

To this extent Stephens's earth is a version of Blake's Ulro as distinct from his Beulah.

But Stephens's thought diverges sharply from that of Blake when the sex relationship appears in its eternal manifestation. Finaun's story in *The Demi-Gods*—briefly to anticipate again—traces the war of the sexes from genesis to apocalypse,[25] and in that account the struggle between the two forces is presented as basic to all life, earthly and celestial. Blake's view of eternity is one with St Matthew's : 'In Eternity they neither marry nor are given in marriage,'[26] and 'Sexes must vanish & cease to be when Albion arises from his dread repose.'[27]

Stephens's view draws on Blake especially in its sense of the archetypal, but it draws more fully on the teaching of the theosophists and their doctrine of polarities. The Theosophists, specifically Madame Blavatsky in *The Secret Doctrine*, saw creation as a tension of opposing forces : from the interaction of night and day, darkness and light, evil and good, man and woman, the universal energies are generated. The world is in a constant state of ebb and flow, action and reaction. On the human level the most vivid function of these polar energies is the sexual drive, the struggle between man and woman for love or supremacy, a struggle which has a whole series of cosmic parallels and equivalents. Just as 'The Red-Haired Man's Wife' and 'Nora Crionna' dramatised this restless struggle in earthly, domestic terms, another of the vision poems presents it in one of its cosmic manifestations. 'Nucleolus' opens with a picture of two divine personages seated on ivory thrones above the world.[28] In a significant phrase they are described as the 'very parallels of grace'. They are thus not joined in love but parallel and separate. The woman asks the man to tell 'the secret, hidden well' which he never has uttered, and promises in return to divulge her own 'guarded thought' :

> Then He—When those who kneel beside
> My holy altar do not bear
> A gift, I turn my face aside
> And do not listen to the prayer;
> But whoso brings a gift shall see
> The proof of Me—

> And She—When, on a festal day,
> Youth kneels by youth before my shrine,
> I think, if he or he might lay
> A ruddy cheek to mine,
> And comfort my sick soul, I'd lay
> My crown away.

The poem's most immediate sense concerns the difference between the two secrets. The male desires homage and insists on the exercise of power. The woman desires love and in return for it is willing to relinquish her power. She is the heavenly parallel of the red-haired man's wife. In revealing her secret she is covertly appealing to the male for love. Then the parallels upon which they are fixed might converge. As the poem ends with the revelation of her secret, with no response from him, we must see their predicament as the celestial pattern for earthly love and its failure.[29] It is essential, however, to note that in the first line the poet 'looked from Mount Derision' at this heavenly tableau. Their posture and dialogue must to that extent be seen in the light of irony. Thus Stephens while noting the opposition of the sexes and seeing it as a *datum* of existence does not necessarily assent to it. The challenge of intersexual communication must be met. Our struggle to meet the challenge furnishes the comedy and tragedy of existence.

Through that struggle the exhilarating energies of the world are released and fuelled. Thus the poem was first entitled 'Nucleolus' a word based on the theosophical term 'nucleole' which means 'The Spheres of Being, or Centres of Life',[30] in their 'eternal' and inscrutable aspect, from which men and animals are bred. For his *Collected Poems* Stephens changed the title to 'The Nucleus' thus shedding the more esoteric connotations of his theme and presenting it as a more central and universal poetic statement. The further significance of the change is that Stephens ultimately made his own use of his sources. He absorbed from Blake and Blavatsky those patterns of myth, doctrine and symbology which responded to the charge of his own creative talent and made an imaginative world recognisably and vividly his own. In the prose fantasy this world comes most fully and elaborately into being.

3

The Crock of Gold

The Apocalyptic Form

Critics of Stephens have been content to classify *The Crock of Gold* as 'prose fantasy' on the perfectly valid grounds that it is not realistic fiction, that it creates for its purposes a fantasy world with its own laws or its own indigenous anarchies. It is a convenient label—and has been used as such in the present study in several passing references to the book—but it has two disabilities. It tends to associate *The Crock of Gold* with the children's fantasies of English writers such as Kenneth Grahame and Walter de la Mare whose methods and intentions were sharply different from those of Stephens. It distracts, in a limiting way, from the serious dimensions of satire, allegory and prophesy which give the book its richness of intellectual content and artistic wholeness. It is therefore more fruitful to approach the book in terms of its natural antecedents, the prophetic poems of Blake and, more immediately, the apocalyptic stories of Yeats.

Blake's prophetic poems, notably 'The Four Zoas', dramatise the dissolution of the human personality in his peculiar version of the Fall, and forecast the ultimate reunion of its faculties and members in a final apocalyptic vision. We have Stephens's word for it that he conceived of *The Crock of Gold* in similar terms:

> In this book there is only one character—Man—Pan is his sensual nature, Caitilin, his emotional nature, the Philosopher his intellect at play, Angus Og his intellect spiritualised, the policemen his conventions and logics, the leprecauns his elemental side, the children his innocence, and the idea is not too rigidly carried out, but that is how I conceived the story.[1]

The rhetorical structure of the fable can be seen as a sort of allegory in which the human faculties are, at the outset of the story, dislocated, and are finally reunited in the apocalyptic flourish with which the book ends.

This pattern in which the ancient pagan gods, classical and Celtic, are represented as awakening and returning to Ireland to be the catalysts of a new dispensation, had already found expression in the occasional writings of AE and in the *Secret Rose* stories of Yeats. A passage from AE, with which Stephens would have been familiar, appears in *The Irish Theosophist*, March-April, 1895 under the title of 'The Ancient Legends of Ireland' :

> The Golden Age is all about us, and heroic forms and imperishable love. In that mystic light rolled round our hills and valleys hang deeds and memories which yet live and inspire. The Gods have not deserted us. Hearing our call they will return. A new cycle is dawning and the sweetness of the morning twilight is in the air. We can breathe it as if we can but awaken from our slumber.

Yeats, in 'Rosa Alchemica', the culminating story of his volume, *The Secret Rose*, as it first appeared in 1897, gives the following lines to his Rosicrucian, Michael Robartes :

> "A time will come for these people also, and they will sacrifice a mullet to Artemis, or some other fish to some new divinity, unless indeed their own divinities, the Dagda, with his overflowing cauldron, Lu, with his spear dipped in poppy-juice ... Angus, with the three birds on his shoulder, Bove and his red swine-herd, and all the heroic children of Dana set up once more their temples of grey stone.'[2]

I have argued at more length elsewhere[3] that *The Secret Rose* is organised in its entirety around a concept of apocalyptic structure: that each of the stories ends in a 'thrust into the numinous' and that the book as a whole moves through 'twenty centuries of stony sleep' towards the birth of a new Dionysiac dispensation involving the return of the old gods. Stephens's version of apocalypse differs in many respects from those of Russell and Yeats. It is presented in the idiom of comedy, and sometimes of conscious parody. Yeats's prophesy is solemn and terrible, whereas Stephens's is exultant, humorous and optimistic. But it shares with both Yeats and Russell a vision of a world transformed by the return of ancient, magical and elemental forces represented by the pagan gods.

Parody and Satire

To write of satire and parody in *The Crock of Gold* is to risk giving them excessive prominence within its organisation. The purpose in raising them at this early stage of the discussion is at once to get them out of the way, and to create an awareness of their presence in the unfolding of the book's overall narrative strategy. The book's *genre* is that of the pastoral idyll, and the patterns of satire, parody and apocalypse are ultimately subsumed into that form and mode. Its setting is that of an Irish Arcadia and its heroine, in accordance with the pastoral convention, is a shepherdess, living in a state of primal innocence with nature. In the book's last sentence where the Philosopher returns to 'the country of the gods' that innocent pastoral world finally triumphs; Eden is restored. The book therefore fulfils Schiller's famous definition of the idyll as that literary form which 'presents the idea and description of an innocent and happy humanity' :

> A state such as this is not merely met with before the dawn of civilisation; it is also the state to which civilisation aspires, as to its last end, if only it obeys a determined tendency in its progress. The idea of a similar state, and the belief in the possible reality of this state, is the only thing that can reconcile man with all the evils to which he is exposed in the path of civilisation . . .[4]

Stephens, who perhaps never read Schiller, put forward a similar view in a letter to Drinkwater already quoted in the Introduction :

> I believe that everything the best mind of humanity really wishes for, and formulates the wish, must come to pass. So I look on certain abstract words such as 'love', 'honour', 'spirit', as prophetic words, having no concrete existence now, but to be forged in the future by the desire which has sounded them. Poems, too, are to me prophesies, and there will be a gay old sometime.[5]

The Crock of Gold is written in this spirit of passionate desire. By an intense imagining the writer brings the 'gay old world' into figurative existence, and by the same process brings closer its actual possibility. Stephens's apocalypse is therefore at one with Schiller's concept of 'aspiration' and Blake's assertion that his own work was 'an Endeavour to Restore what the Ancients call'd the Golden Age'.[6] Stephens's work makes a similar act of faith in human possibility. He does not appeal for our belief in the actual existence of his gods and fairies but for the possibilities of love, innocence and energy which they symbolise.

AE believed in the objective existence of the Celtic gods and in the imminence of their return. Yeats's belief in them is notoriously problematical, but in his three 'apocalyptic' stories, 'Rosa Alchemica', 'The Tables of the Law' and 'The Adoration of the Magi', their return is treated without irony as a terrible and immediate threat to contemporary civilisation. In this context the parodic element in *The Crock of Gold* becomes evident.

Some fifteen years before its publication Yeats and Russell, together with MacGregor Mathers, William Sharp ('Fiona MacLeod'), Maud Gonne and others, had been active in the founding of a cult of 'Celtic Paganism'. Convinced that the gods of the Tuatha de Danaan were about to return to Ireland they had attempted to set up a religion based on the old Celtic mysteries as interpreted in the light of Theosophy and Rosicrucianism. They had sought out a castle on an island in Lough Key, in County Sligo, which was to be their temple. They believed that a Celtic 'Avatar' or redeemer had already been born and was at hand—if he could be found—to preside over the movement. In a letter to Yeats of February, 1896, Russell assured Yeats that

> The gods have returned to Erin and have centred themselves in the sacred mountains and blow the fires through the land. They have been seen by several in vision, they will awaken the magical instinct everywhere, and the universal heart of the people will turn to the old druidic beliefs. . . . I believe profoundly that a new Avatar is about to appear . . . It will be one of the kingly Avatars, who is at once ruler of men and magic sage.[7]

Yeats set himself to draw up a ritual for the proposed cult, and it is significant in the present context that the chief god was to be Aengus, symbolising 'Spiritual Intelligence'. In *The Crock of*

Gold Angus stands for 'the intellect spiritualised'. The attempt to establish the cult failed,[8] and when *The Crock of Gold* came to be written was little more than an exotic and perhaps bizarre memory. It seems certain that Stephens had it in mind when he brought back Pan and Angus to Ireland, the comic landscape of his fantasy; and that his attitude towards them lacked the solemnity of his elders. He was the first of the Irish writers to treat the Celtic gods and heroes irreverently and is thus the fore-runner of a burlesque tradition in Irish fiction that later includes Joyce, Eimar O'Duffy and Flann O'Brien. Parody of Yeats and Russell is not a central ingredient of *The Crock of Gold* but it provides, as we shall see, a delicate and playful flavour to the book's more essential concerns.

The element of satire in the book arises chiefly in the counter-point of the rural idyll of endless freedom against the city with its prisons, laws and repressions. When the book was first published it was compared to Goldsmith's *Vicar of Wakefield*. The comparison is apt because Goldsmith was the first writer in English to effect a conjunction of traditional pastoral with the novel form. *The Vicar of Wakefield* draws much of its strength and poignancy from the contrast between the world of rural innocence with its peaceful seasonal patterns and the treacherous world of the towns with their pitfalls for the simple, their arbitrary laws and inhuman prisons. In *The Crock of Gold* a persistent argument goes on between the two worlds. It is at its most overt when the Philosopher is arrested by Policemen for a crime he did not commit, and at its most intense and desolating when, in Chapter XVI, he sits in darkness and listens to the stories of his two cellmates about their persecution by society and its laws. This conflict furnishes one aspect of the book's satirical syndrome: the contrast between the pastoral world where the motions and desires of man are given free and harmonious expression among the rhythms of nature, and the world of social man where these aspirations are repressed and maimed by law and custom. The second, and no less important function of the satire concerns Pan's mission to Ireland, a country where 'no people have done reverence' to him. This prong of the satiric intention is aimed at Ireland's traditional distrust of the passions, its Jansenist and Victorian suspicion of the natural impulses. In this respect Stephens joins Moore, Yeats and Joyce as a critic of the conservative *mores* of contemporary Irish life. Together with the satire on law and justice this criticism of society's attitude to the natural instincts finds expression in the allegorical pattern which traces the fortunes of Caitilin, the Philosopher and the Thin Woman through the book's narrative process.

The Comic Idiom

The Crock of Gold is above all a comic novel. Though all of its fictive characters may stand for separate human faculties they must also put on flesh and become believable human personalities. To achieve this verisimilitude Stephens had to find a narrative idiom which would suspend disbelief and persuade the reader of a lived reality while, at the same time, making sure that the doctrinal implications of the fable would not drop altogether from sight.

He begins therefore with a narrative convention that is fabulous, proverbial, gnomic: 'In the centre of the pine wood called Coilla Doraca there lived not long ago two Philosophers.' The narrative voice assumes the privileges of the Irish 'seanchai' (traditional story-teller) and places the action at a suitable distance in time and space, somewhere between myth and history, between Eliade's *hoc tempus* and *illud tempus*.[9] If the message is to be Blakean the setting will be radically Stephensian, a world which can accommodate not only Pan and Angus Og, but policemen, tinkers, leprecauns, resurrected heroes and arguments about lumps in the porridge. Magic, mystery and miracle are fused with the quotidian and the domestic: the Philosopher's ministry is, as we are told at the opening of Chapter II, to give advice to people 'on subjects too recondite for even those extremes of elucidation, the parish priest and the tavern'. The chief catalyst between the human and the numinous is the comic. The book, like *The Charwoman's Daughter*, employs the traditional comic plot: its heroine eludes the constraints of prudence and of parental sanction to achieve marriage with the youthful god, Angus Og. In doing so she not only transcends the dry morality of the Philosopher but becomes instrumental in his conversion to those values of joy, spontaneity and fertility which he had so strenuously distrusted. On the human level the book's rhetorical trend affirms these traditional comic values against the sterile constraints of established social *mores*. The book's *dramatis personae* are drawn from the comedy of humours: the naïve heroine, the bumbling policeman, the mischievous fairy, the droll countryman, the absent-minded philosopher plagued by his practical and shrewish wife—perhaps a deliberate echo of Socrates and Xanthippé. But here the comic action works itself out in consistent patterns of allegory and the comic ending passes on into happy apocalypse.

That the two Philosophers, despite their prodigious learning, do not know everything, is deftly suggested in the first chapter when it appears that they cannot account for the simultaneous birth of a boy and a girl to their wives. Logic is their thinking instrument and their home is a dark wood; the marvel of fertility is beyond them. By the end of the first chapter their children have discovered the sun. By the end of the second one of the Philosophers has died because he 'has attained to all the wisdom he is fitted to bear'. Before he goes his brother informs him of certain things that he has not mastered—'how to play the tambourine, nor how to be nice to your wife, nor how to get up first in the morning and cook the breakfast ... how to smoke strong tobacco' or 'dance in the moonlight with a woman of the Shee'. For his own part he concludes that perhaps 'the ultimate end is gaiety and music and a dance of joy'. The brother is not deterred; but it is also true that the surviving Philosopher makes no attempt to put his own theories into practice. He continues to talk and cerebrate and infuriate his wife. His enlightenment and transformation forms the main allegorical strand in the book's pattern; the flowering and development of Caitilin's womanhood forms the next; the pilgrimage of the Thin Woman fills out the third. But as Caitilin's development precipitates all of the others —including those of the minor characters and that of Angus Og himself—it is best to begin with her role in the fable.

Caitilin's Progress

Caitilin, like Mary Makebelieve, is introduced at the moment when her sexuality is beginning to announce itself. Like Blake's Thel she is a virginal shepherdess poised on the brink of experience. Unlike Thel she does not recoil from the reality of sex, nor, like Oothoon, is she delivered over to the forces of morality and convention. Instead, through the good offices of Pan and Angus she is granted in the end a joyful progress to full womanhood.

From the outset she is seen as having an especial affinity with nature as she moves among the vegetation and the animals in a mood of 'warm thoughtlessness' :

Indeed everything in her quiet world loved this girl : but very slowly there was growing in her consciousness an unrest, a disquietude to which she had hitherto been a stranger. Sometimes an infinite weariness oppressed her to the earth. A thought was born in her mind and it had no name. It was growing and could not be expressed. She had no words wherewith to meet it, to exorcise or greet this stranger who, more and more insistently and pleadingly, tapped upon her doors and begged to be spoken to, admitted and caressed and nourished.

This stranger, her instinctive desire for sexual fulfilment, approaches first through the half-heard music of Pan, then through the discernible melody of his pipes 'full of austerity and aloofness', and finally through the apparition of the god himself. The process is subtly managed in its early gradations and it moves towards a confrontation as dramatic as Mary's with the Policeman's eye :

The upper part of his body was beautiful, but the lower part ... She dared not look at him again. She would have risen and fled away but she feared he might pursue, and the thought of such a chase and the inevitable capture froze her blood.

The skill with which Stephens has dramatised the girl's state of mind anchors the experience in the world of psychological reality. Simultaneously, of course, the moment is heightened by the presence of older, more archetypal versions of the situation, the fables of Pan and Syrinx, of Cupid and Psyche.

When Pan speaks to her Caitilin first takes refuge in the conventional response : 'I will do whatever you say is right.' Pan dismisses the concept urging instead the Blakean imperative of desire : 'You must not do anything because it is right, but because it is your wish.' As he proceeds with his argument—half homily, half seduction—he refashions the Philosopher's earlier propositions on wisdom and love :

The name of the heights is Wisdom and the name of the

depths is Love. How shall they come together and be fruitful if you do not plunge deeply and fearlessly? Wisdom is the spirit and the wings of the spirit, Love is the shaggy beast that goes down. Gallantly he dives, below thought, beyond Wisdom, to rise again as high above these as he had first descended.

When Caitilin consents to go with him it is in response not to her intellect but her heart, 'because he was naked and alone'. It is clear that Pan was too experienced in the rhetoric of love to have made the mistake of the Red-Haired Man or the Policeman.

A consistent feature of Stephens's narrative strategy is the counterpoint of the solemn against the whimsical, the momentous against the commonplace, the cosmic against the domestic. Pan's wooing of Caitilin, accordingly, is followed by her father's comic embassy to the Philosopher for help in getting her back. Here, as the Philosopher weaves his way intricately towards a solution, and as Meehawl with a sort of droll patience tries to keep him to the point, the abduction is at once annotated and placed in the mundane perspective of kitchen comedy. Two kinds of discourse are played off against each other in humorous counterpoint while patterns of literary parody and social satire are fed into the structure. Meehawl's rustic idiom constantly picks up Synge's dramatic dialogue :

'Did you ever hear', said Meehawl, 'of the man that had the scalp of his head blown off by a gun, and they soldered the bottom of a tin dish to the top of his skull the way you could hear his brains ticking inside of it for all the world like a Waterby watch.'[10]

Similarly the expectations of Yeats and Russell of a Celtic Avatar are gently mocked in the dialogue that follows. The Philosopher's assertion that Pan had never visited Ireland and that 'his coming intends no good to this country' is an obvious comment on the sexual puritanism of contemporary Ireland which so many writers of the Revival had been consistently satirising.

Having identified the abductor as Pan, the Philosopher explains to Meehawl that Pan has power over all grown people to make them 'fall in love with every person they meet, and commit assaults and things I wouldn't like to be telling you about'.

He resolves to send his two children to treat with the god and to tell him 'he isn't doing the decent thing'. If this ploy fails, the Celtic god, Angus Og, is to be their last resource :

> 'He'd make short work of him, I'm thinking.'
> 'He might surely; but he may take the girl for himself all the same.'
> 'Well, I'd sooner he had her than the other one, for he's one of ourselves anyhow, and the devil you know is better than the devil you don't know.'
> 'Angus Og is a god,' said the Philosopher severely.

From this point forward the Philosopher and Caitilin are set upon parallel courses : both come under the sensual influence of Pan and both proceed, by different paths, to human completion under the influence of Angus Og, the 'intellect spiritualised'. The children's embassy to Pan having failed, the Philosopher sets out to invoke the aid of the Irish god. His encounter with Pan by the way is provoked by the sight of Caitilin, naked and unashamed, in the fields by the Greek god's cave. His disputation with Pan is a battle of polarities in which he is defeated, comically, not by the god's logic but by the music of his pipes, which strike at his hitherto undeveloped sexual faculties :

> 'You leave out the new thing,' said the Philosopher. 'You leave out brains. I believe in mind above matter. Thought above emotion. Spirit above flesh.'
> 'Of course you do,' said Pan, and he reached for his oaten pipe. The Philosopher ran to the opening of the passage and thrust Caitilin aside.
> 'Hussy,' said he fiercely to her, and he darted out. As he went up the rugged path he could hear the pipes of Pan, calling and sobbing and making high merriment on the air.

The Philosopher's Progress

Chapter XI of Book Two takes the Philosopher from the cave of Pan to the dwelling of Angus Og, and as he proceeds a series of changes and recognitions take place in his psyche. He begins with a wilful adherence to his previous ethical imperatives : ' "She does not deserve to be rescued," said the Philosopher, "but I will rescue her. Indeed," he thought a moment later, "she does not want to be rescued, and, *therefore*, I will rescue her." ' The servant of Urizen dies hard, but his three encounters on the journey guarantee the birth of the new man. Haunted by the naked beauty of Caitilin, and in obedience to an unprecedented impulse, he kisses a fat woman by the way. He offers sympathy to an old beggarwoman and is witness to her humiliation at the hands of settled society.[11] As yet he is unable to relieve her distress : Pan has, by irrigating his sexual instincts, aroused the capacity for sympathy; but the influence of Angus Og is necessary before that faculty can blossom into active and effective charity. Thirdly, he becomes involved with a tinker band who wish him to marry their woman and thus resolve their difficulties. The tinkers are refugees from Synge, problematically involved with a social institution alien to their freebooting way of life. The Philosopher refuses to be conscripted, escapes under cover of darkness, and soon finds himself bowing before the godhead of Angus. Here the two main allegorical strands meet again : at the Philosopher's request Angus proceeds to Pan's cave to claim Caitilin; the Philosopher, renewed by the Divine Imagination of Angus, sets out on his momentous journey home.

The contention of the gods for the love of Caitilin is, significantly, a trial not of strength but of weakness, of need. Caitilin had gone with Pan because he had been naked and alone. She chooses Angus because his need is greater. His plea is similar to that of Pan—and it recalls Pan's earlier complaint that 'in this country no people have done any reverence to me' :

'I want you,' said Angus Og, 'because the world has forgotten me. In all my nation there is no remembrance of me. I, wandering the hills of my country, am lonely indeed. . . . Thought has snared my birds in his nets and sold them in the market-places.'

It is hardly fanciful to detect in these sentences the voice of the Irish Literary Renaissance pleading for the values of poetry and imagination against the materialism and philistinism of the age. And as he proceeds Angus invokes the larger perspectives of Blake and his aspiration of human wholeness : 'Lo, I am sealed in the caves of nonentity until the head and the heart shall come together in fruitfulness, until Thought has wept for Love, and Emotion has purified herself to meet her lover. Tir-na-nOg is the heart of a man and the head of a woman.'[12] Union with a mortal woman rescues the god from non-entity. Caitilin becomes the bridgehead from which the Immortals can reconquer Ireland and re-establish Tir-na-nOg. Analogously Caitilin, the human *tabula rasa* upon whim the gods can write their intentions, has progressed from unthinking virginity through awakened sensuality to completion by union with the Divine Imagination of Angus Og. The stage is being set for the final apocalyptic climax of the book's action.

The Philosopher's homeward journey is marked by a two-fold pattern. His state of well-being now issues in overt acts of humanity and loving-kindness, and each of these acts becomes the occasion for his message of regeneration. He offers to share his bread with a bearded man and his sons, and in the exchange of hospitality that follows he discovers that the man is Mac Cul. He comforts the love-lorn girl and discovers that her lover is Mac-Culain. He proffers food to a boy and it is revealed that the boy is named Mac-Cushin. To each of them—clearly versions of the Irish heroes, Fionn, Cu Chulain and Oisin—he delivers Angus's message that the 'Sleepers of Erinn' are about to awaken. But before the apocalypse can take place the allegory has a number of intricate strands to unwind.

The role of the sub-plot, from which the novel takes its name, does not become apparent until the Philosopher returns and is arrested by policemen for the alleged murder of his brother and sister-in-law. The leprecauns have given false evidence against him because in helping Meehawl to recover his washboard he had been unwittingly responsible for the loss of their crock of gold. The leprecauns, as we have seen, are elementals, and therefore have no morality. When they lose their crock of gold they kidnap the Philosopher's children, but when the Thin Woman threatens them with her fairy relatives they give them back. When the children return their gold they try to make amends by ambushing the Policemen and rescuing the Philosopher on his way to prison. They are perhaps best seen as part of the novel's 'machinery'—a sort of earthy version of Pope's sylphs—and their function at this stage of the fable is twofold. They throw open the way for the Philosopher to submit deliberately to the law, and to deliver himself formally to the Policemen's custody. They provide the opportunity for the Thin Woman to undertake her

pilgrimage to Angus Og by first performing the Blakean sacra-
ment of the 'Forgiveness of Enemies':[13]

Before the Thin Woman could undertake the redemption of
her husband by wrath, it was necessary that she should be
purified by the performance of that sacrifice which is called
the Forgiveness of Enemies, and this she did by embracing the
Leprechauns of the Gort and in the presence of the sun and
the wind remitting their crime against her husband. Thus she
became free to devote her malice against the State of Punishment, while forgiving the individuals who had but acted in
obedience to the pressure of their infernal environment, which
pressure is Sin.[14]

The Philosopher is about to enter upon his final purgatorial
experience. He is still the book's sturdy champion of the mind.
From the story's outset he had dwelt in the darkness of Coilla
Doraca, 'the Dark Woods', and there he had asserted the stamina
and indomitability of the intellect over darkness, limitation,
human perplexity. In the spiritual adventure of meeting the two
gods his mind had been enriched by imagination and love. Now,
more than ever, when the Policemen arrest him, he feels confident of the power of mind over matter, of innocence over the
hostile world of law and custom. So, as he is borne through
the darkness by the police, there is meaning as well as absurdity
in his indefatigable monologues on ants, birds and policemen. In
these the free mind refuses to be silenced by the truncheons of
retributive justice. When, after his rescue and his stirabout, he
resolves to give himself up, he does so in obedience to a conviction that is admirable, but which the fable's action is to reveal
as mistaken:

'An innocent man', said he, 'cannot be oppressed, for he is
fortified by his mind and his heart cheers him. It is only on a
guilty person that the rigour of punishment can fall, for he
punishes himself. That is what I think, that a man should
always obey the law with his body and always disobey it with
his mind. I have been arrested, the men of law had me in their
hands, and I will have to go back to them so that they may do
whatever they have to do.

The humour with which the Philosopher's arrival at the police station is related, the confusion and delight of the policeman on duty, the hospitality of the Sergeant and of Shawn seeing him on the morrow, can easily deflect us from the serious implications of the action. What is being urged upon us is the conviction that the mind of man cannot, despite its best efforts and purest intentions, triumph over an organised system of social restraint and punitive justice. The Philosopher is permitted by his relieved and beaming captors to wander in the prison yard and 'smoke until he was black in the face'. There he finds himself mourning with the sweet pea on its wretched existence and congratulating the nasturtium 'on its two bright children'. Gradually the reality of imprisonment begins to oppress him : he finds himself exclaiming, 'Indeed, poor creatures ... ye also are in gaol.' And when he returns to his cell he is possessed of a blackness 'both within and without'. It is a poignant moment in the book when this sterling exponent of the free intellect finds himself asking : 'Can one's mind go to prison as well as one's body?' It is as he faces this new and unnerving possibility that the two prisoners' stories are brilliantly interpolated.

Both prisoners had been clerks, obedient servants of society, but now are thieves and outlaws. Misfortune had come to one through sickness, to the other through age. Both had been put out of their employment with no means of livelihood. The first had taken to the road because he had been afraid to face his starving wife and family, the other because he could no longer pay the rent. Both stories are rehearsed in total darkness, symbolic of the unredeemed city ruled over by 'the dark People of the Fomor'[15] later indicted in the 'Happy March' with which the book triumphantly ends. The stories serve to define the aridity and injustice of the urban world and to bring it into sharp contrast with the sunlit, fertile world of gods and fairies which the Philosopher has so recently vacated. They foreshadow for us the fate in store for the hero if the Thin Woman cannot enlist the help of the gods to effect his rescue. As the second prisoner falls silent the section ends :

When the morning came the Philosopher was taken on a car to the big City in order that he might be put on trial and hanged. It was the custom.

The Thin Woman's Ordeal

Though the influence of Blake has been frequently invoked in discussing the novel so far the fable can be perfectly enjoyed without any reference to the English poet. The use of prose narrative frees Stephens from the intrusion of Blake's style; the comic idiom, the Irish setting and *dramatis personae* give free play to the originality of Stephens's genius. And the relevant areas of Blake's thought have been so thoroughly absorbed by Stephens that they merge easily into the elaborate narrative pattern of the fantasy. Indeed the plea for sexual freedom, for the primacy of impulse and the sense of polar tension between male and female might be justly claimed as a foreshadowing of Lawrence rather than as a derivation from Blake.

But there is one episode in *The Crock of Gold* which would be hard to account for without formal reference to Blake's symbolic system, and that is the Thin Woman's encounter with the Three Absolutes in Book VI, Chapter XVII. This is the least successful phase of the novel. These three massive naked men who challenge the Thin Woman as she makes her way with her children to the cave of Angus are in every sense intruders. We have not met them before, we are not clear as to their intentions—the Thin Woman is hardly an object of spontaneous desire—and we feel the need to cast around for their backgrounds and identity.

Here immediately we recognise them as shadowy visitors from Blake. Hilary Pyle, for a start, is clearly right in identifying them as the Three Britons who escaped after the last Battle of King Arthur as related in Blake's *Descriptive Catalogue* of 1809,[16] and in associating them further with three of Blake's Zoas, Urizen, Luvah and Tharmas. Her exegesis may, however, be taken a little further. Urizen whom Stephens rightly associates with Thought—and plausibly with Beauty—offers the Thin Woman immunity from 'all raging passions' and from the 'gross' demands of the flesh. On the fictional level the offer is a little incongruous. Lust has not been one of her besetting sins and she is anything but a sex object : we recall that when the Philosopher had urged her to approach Pan at the opening of Book II he had pointed out 'that her age, her appearance, and her tongue were sufficient guarantees of immunity against the machinations of either Pan or slander'. Her reply to Urizen is as bald and simple as Bartleby's, she chooses not to, and he cannot compel her. He acquiesces. The incident is not psychologically satisfying as fiction : as allegory it can be defended on the grounds that her married life has entered into a new phase of love and tenderness, and that she has already, by the 'Forgiveness of Sins', freed herself from the more predominant of her 'raging passions', anger.

Luvah, properly associated with Love—and again plausibly with Strength—offers the Thin Woman peace and love under the protection of that strength. Her answer is that as a mother her 'strength cannot be increased', her love 'cannot be added to'. Tharmas, rightly identified with Lust—rather arbitrarily with Ugliness—offers her everything that is 'crude and riotous, all that is gross and without limit'. His appeal, perhaps because it is made to the side of her nature that she has most consistently denied, proves hardest for the Thin Woman to resist. Significantly it is 'the hands of the children' that 'withheld her while in woe she abased herself before him'. Her answer is twofold : that it is not lawful 'to turn again when the journey is commenced', which can refer to the journey through life or the pilgrimage to Angus Og; and secondly that 'the torments of the mind may not be renounced for any easement of the body until the smoke that blinds us is blown away, and the tormenting flame has fitted us for that immortal ecstasy which is the bosom of God.' Like the other replies it is both cryptic and perfunctory and not strikingly to the point. None of the answers has the felicity or ingenuity found in the many folk tales where this sort of challenge is offered to the traveller. Taken as a whole the incident can be seen as the Thin Woman's refusal to have her faculties separated. She must cling to her psychic integrity until she too has found Angus. He stands for the fourth Zoa, Los or Urthona : through and with him the other three are to be reunited to form the perfect human person.

The Celtic Apocalypse

The books ends on a note of triumphant apocalypse in which the motifs of allegory, satire and literary parody are given a final orchestration. As they prepare for the 'Happy March' on the city to rescue the Philosopher—'the Intellect of Man'—Angus announces to Caitilin that there will be a second journey from which they will not return, 'for we will live among our people and be at peace' :

c

'May the day come soon,' said she.

'When thy son is a man he will go before us on that journey,' said Angus, and Caitilin shivered with a great delight, knowing that a son would be born to her.

Russell's Avatar is clearly in the womb of time. Accordingly the return of the old Celtic gods is at hand. On their second visit to the city we presume that Dublin—like Blake's London—will be redeemed and transfigured. But for the moment, in accordance with the spirit of pastoral comedy, the celebratory close of the story will have its setting amid the peace of nature, in 'the country of the gods'.

As the dormant hosts of fairy Ireland descend upon the city their song gathers together the entirety of the book's themes, the prison of urban society, the tyranny of law, convention and morality, the slavery of the factory and the counting house, and the contrary values of freedom, spontaneity, sexual love and poetic imagination. The song's refrain ingeniously echoes lines from a poem by Yeats and one by AE: in 'The Hosting of the Sidhe' Yeats evokes 'Caoilte tossing his burning hair' and Niamh calling 'Away, come away,' while AE's poem 'Content' ends

> Come away, O, come away;
> We will quench the heart's desire
> Past the gateways of the day
> In the rapture of the fire.

Thus Stephens's victorious chant is at once a summary and a culmination to the book's rhetorical intention:

> Come away! Come away! from the loom and the desk, from the shop where the carcasses are hung, from the place where raiment is sold and sewn in darkness: O bad treachery! Is it for joy you sit in the broker's den, thou pale man? Has the attorney enchanted thee? . . . Come away! for the dance has begun lightly, the wind is sounding over the hill . . .

The book's last flourish comes through the narrative voice where Blakean rhetoric, Irish myth, and a wry note of comedy are blended into the pattern, and the allegory enacts its last gesture:

> And they took the Philosopher from his prison, even the Intellect of Man they took from the hands of the doctors and

the lawyers, from the sly priests, from the professors whose mouths are gorged with sawdust, and the merchants who sell blades of grass—the awful people of the Fomor . . . and then they returned again, dancing and singing, to the country of the gods . . .

4

The Stephens Short Story

Journalism into Fiction

The short fiction of James Stephens grew out of his journalism, and the short stories that make up his first volume, *Here Are Ladies*, show clear traces of their origins. His writing career had begun with a short story in *The United Irishman* in 1905. Two years later, in April 1907, he began his association with Griffith's paper, *Sinn Féin*. There all his prose pieces were published until April 1911, when the first instalment of *The Charwoman's Daughter* appeared in *The Irish Review* under the title, 'Mary, a Story'. These contributions to *Sinn Féin* divide roughly into three categories: nationalistic articles with such titles as 'The Seoinin', 'Irish Englishmen', 'On the Viceregal Microbe'; then whimsical sketches, 'On Washing', 'On Shaving', 'On Eating', mostly spoken by his fictional persona, the Old Philosopher;[1] finally, short fictional sketches such as 'Miss Arabella Hennessy', 'Mrs Larry Tracy', 'Old Mrs Hannigan', 'The Man who was Afraid'. The subsequent fate of these pieces is a matter of literary curiosity which throws a good deal of light on Stephens's creative procedures. The last two titles mentioned, for instance, found their way into his novel, *The Crock of Gold*.[2] The two previous, with slight alterations, were included as stories in *Here Are Ladies*. The reflections of the Old Philosopher were gathered under the title 'There is a Tavern in the Town', and as such take up the last seventy pages of *Here Are Ladies*. Passages from them are used as dialogue for the Philosopher in *The Crock of Gold*. It all adds up to a dashing exercise in literary economy. Details of the shifts and transferences are available in Birgit Bramsbäck's bibliographical study of 1959.[3]

Had the short story volume *Here Are Ladies* appeared as Stephens had first planned it the result would have been casual and uneven. Even its final form is not very distinguished, though it is better organised than most short story collections. When he conceived it, Stephens was short of money. He had given up his clerical job in Dublin and taken his family to live in Paris. The first manuscript of the book submitted did not contain the more mature stories of the final volume—'A Glass of Beer', 'The Triangle', 'The Threepenny-Piece', 'The Horses', 'The Blind Man'. These were added in response to a request from the publisher in April 1913 for extra material to bring the book up to 60,000 words.[4] In meeting the request Stephens saw the possibility of giving the book a structural coherence which it had not so far achieved. And what makes the final volume such a pleasant book to read is the shrewdness with which its component pieces —often thin and unsubstantial in themselves—are deployed within its structure. The pattern, which recurs five times in the volume is as follows: a poem announcing a theme; a triad of sketches exploring the theme in three different situations; an independent story dramatising the theme in more depth and greater extension. The book's main structure, therefore, may be indicated thus:

Poem	Triad	Story
'Women'	'Three Heavy Husbands'	'A Glass of Beer'
'One and One'	'Three Women who Wept'	'The Triangle'
'The Daisies'	'Three Angry People'	'The Threepenny Piece'
'Brigid'	'Three Young Wives'	'The Horses'
'Mistress Quiet Eyes'	'Three Lovers who Lost'	'The Blind Man'

The pattern peters out towards the end where the short story yields to the non-fictional sketch. Thus the poem, 'Sweet Apple' is followed by a triad of sketches; a poem entitled 'The Moon' follows, and the book ends with that succession of monologues already referred to, 'There is a Tavern in the Town'. If the volume had not been so hurriedly assembled it is likely that Stephens would have hacked away the dead wood at the end and achieved a consistent pattern throughout.

To Stephens, student of Hermes, disciple of AE and reader of Blavatsky, three was a magical number: there are three words in the title—his first suggestion had been *Triangles*—there are triform sections, triadic stories, titles involving triangles and three-penny pieces, stories of lover, rival and beloved. Side by side with the triadic pattern there is the war of the sexes, waged with the same pertinacity as in the dramatic lyrics: the cosmic dualism that has been seen in a poem like 'Nucleolus' is now worked out in the kitchen and the living-room, from story to story, in a restless manoeuvre of opposites. Thus the dualism of the theme is adroitly counterpointed against the trinity of structure as Stephens explores the tensions and ambiguities of inter-sexual relationships inside and outside marriage.

The five extra stories which Stephens provided on the publisher's request are, I would argue, the best stories in the volume. They are the work of a more mature artist, a writer who has come to sense the unique potential of the *genre*. Furthermore, they are not written for the constricting context of a newspaper; they have a sense of liberty, a new amplitude. Each of them is therefore prominently placed in the structure—at the end of a triad and as a sort of culmination to its theme. Stephens's revisions of the early *Sinn Féin* pieces are subtly calculated to assist the book's design. In almost every case the names of the characters are removed; the emphasis shifts unobtrusively from character to theme. Now 'he' and 'she' become agents in an endless interpersonal manoeuvre supervised by the pervasive, and sometimes rather fussy, narrating voice. As a general principle of organisation, therefore, it could be said that in each section the poem states the theme; the triad dramatises it through the actions of impersonal agents; the culminating story re-examines it in terms of more amply articulated character. Thus Stephens transcends the limitations of the material with which he set out and contrives for his book a curious and un-expected coherence.

Theme and Character

It is consonant with the writer's general intentions that, parti-cularly in the triads, he portrays the majority of his human agents in terms of caricature—by the exaggeration of a single feature:

> She was tall and angular. Her hair was red, and scarce, and untidy. Her hands were large and packed all over with knuckles and her feet would have turned inwards at the toes, only that she was aware of and corrected their perversities. . . .

Her voice was pleasant enough but it was so strong that one fancied there were bones in it. ('Three Angry People' III)

The insistence on bones, knuckles and angularity is sufficient to establish a sort of female who will find the dominance of man intolerable.

She had begun to get thin. Her face was growing sharp and peaked. The steady curve of her cheek had become a little indeterminate. Her chin had begun to sag and her eyes to look a little weary. ('Three Women Who Wept' III)

This is all we get in physical description of the heroine, but it is sufficient to establish that she will be sadly vulnerable to a thoughtless young adventurer who seeks sanctuary at her house.

He had a high nose. He looked at one over the collar, so to speak. His regard was very assured, and his speech was the short bundle of monosyllables which the subaltern throws at the orderly. He had never been questioned, and, the precedent being absent, he had never questioned himself. ('Three Heavy Husbands' I)

This is the portrait of a man who will inevitably be betrayed by his attractive wife and cuckolded by his clerk without ever quite understanding what has happened.

He was a silent man. . . . With some reservations he enjoyed listening, but particularly he enjoyed listening to his own thoughts as they trod slowly, but very certainly, to foregone conclusions. ('Three Heavy Husbands' II)

We can appreciate that he is also a man 'doubtful of his ability to cope with, or his endurance to withstand, the extraordinary debate called marriage'.

We therefore learn no more about the characters than is necessary to make their actions meaningful. In turn their actions are rigidly controlled by the narrating voice. Nowhere do we get the sense of characters taking on 'autonomous life'; rather do we get the impression of their being moved around on a chess board in a series of intricate thematic patterns by a garrulous and explanatory author. The approach is at the opposite pole to the scrupu-

lous impersonality of Joyce. On the other hand Stephens exhibits
none of the local, the specifically Irish, concern found in Yeats
and Moore. Stephens's characters are Dubliners, but they might
as easily have been Londoners. It is with the quality of universal
absurdity in their behaviour that he concerns himself. He composes a comedy of the sexes in which the postures are love,
hatred, boredom, jealousy, above all—and it is here that
Stephens shows himself most modern—incommunicable loneliness.

The opening triad, 'Three Heavy Husbands', deals lightly with
three failures of communication between young husbands and
their wives. The story which completes the section, 'A Glass of
Beer', is a desolate scrutiny of the theme in terms of an ageing
widower who has come to Paris on the death of his wife :

> His wife had been dead for over a year. He had hungered,
> he had prayed for her death. He had hated that woman (and
> for how many years !) with a kind of masked ferocity. How
> often he had been tempted to kill her or to kill himself ! How
> often he had dreamed that she had run away from him or that
> he had run away from her ! . . . What unending, slow quarrels
> they had together ! How her voice had droned pitilessly on his
> ears ! She in one room, he in another, and through the open
> door there rolled that unending recitation of woes and
> reproaches, an interminable catalogue of nothings, while he
> sat dumb as a fish, with a mind that smouldered and blazed.[5]

The story unfolds itself through the consciousness of the hero as
he sits by his glass of beer in a pavement café. He orders beer
every day not because he likes it, 'but only because it was not a
difficult thing to ask for'. His timidity still prevents him from
communicating with the world even now when it has become, in
a sense, his oyster. Through his mind the distasteful images of
his married life continue to pass, sometimes with startling
violence : 'He had stood unseen with a hammer, a poker, a razor
in his hand, on tiptoe to do it. A movement, a rush, one silent
rush and it was done ! He had caressed it, rehearsed it, relished
it, and jerked her head back, and hacked, and listened to her
entreaties bubbling through blood !'

This vivid contrast between the public man who cannot summon the courage to ask for a newspaper in French and the

private man stirring his cauldron of bloody fantasy is a persistent one with Stephens in these stories. Marriage is repeatedly seen as a condition of 'quiet desperation', a predicament from which love has altogether departed, leaving its opposite in silent and corrosive mastery. Here the widower's meaningless marriage is thrown into absurd relief by his meaningless liberation. In a city synonymous with freedom he is locked within the burnt-out case of his self, looking out at a world with which he cannot connect, and which therefore becomes an image of his self-hatred:

> Raddled faces with heavy eyes and rouged lips. Ragged lips that had been chewed by every mad dog in the world. What lips there were everywhere! Bright scarlet splashes in dead white faces. Thin red gashes that suggested rat-traps instead of kisses. Bulbous, flabby lips that would wobble and shiver if attention failed them. Lips of a horrid fascination that one looked at and hated and ran to.... Looking at him slyly or boldly, as they passed along, and turned after a while and repassed him, and turned again in endless promenade.

The triad entitled 'Three Lovers Who Lost', later in the volume, handles its theme of defeated love buoyantly enough, leading into 'The Blind Man', a story very like 'A Glass of Beer' in its misogyny, its theme of non-communication between the sexes, its contrast between the inner and the outer man, and finally in the desperate bleakness of its close. 'The Blind Man' has for its hero a youth who is described as 'sex-blind' and therefore unable to respond to the feminine principle. As he matures he grows away from his mother until the two can no longer communicate on any level: '... between her son and herself there was a gulf fixed, spanned by no bridge whatever—there was complete isolation—no boat plied between them at all.' His indifference to womanhood permits him to marry an ugly woman for her farm. Now the female principle takes its revenge. He is cruelly awoken to the world of sexual distinction when he finds himself trapped in a household of slatterns. As in the passages quoted from 'A Glass of Beer' Stephens employs his language and imagery to register a sense of morbid obsession in which the race of women is seen less as a sex or a species than as a sort of disease:

And these were all swathed about with petticoats and shawls. They had no movement. Their feet were like those of no creature he had ever observed. One could hear the flip flap of their slippers all over the place, and at all hours. They were down-at-heel, draggle-tailed, and futile. There was no workmanship about them. They were as unfinished, as unsightly as a puddle on a road. They insulted his eyesight, his hearing, and his energy. They had lank hair that slapped about them like wet sea-weed, and they were all talking, talking, talking.

As the story ends the blind man of the title is coming closer to a state of murderous desperation in which we feel that he will do what the lonely widower of 'A Glass of Beer' had so often imagined in terms of fantasy. Both stories represent the darker side of Stephens's creative imagination, that area of his consciousness where he approached a vision of human pain, futility and absurdity foreshadowing the Sartre of *Nausea,* the Beckett of *Molloy.*

In fact what we see happening in *Here Are Ladies* is a writer grappling with a new literary form, the realistic modern short story, coming to terms with it, and then straining beyond it. As his literary progress so far suggests, Stephens is by nature not a realist but a fabulist. He is not attracted by the patient elaboration and annotation of human relationships within the social context. Here we see him transform his juvenilia in the realist short story into fictional patterns wherein characters are transformed into active human principles, dominant and often obsessive states of mind. Sociological décor is largely elided or ignored. Where it is allowed, in 'The Triangle' or 'The Horses', it is only as an arena for the urgent human drives which resent it. The husband in the former remains willingly trapped within it as the story closes. The husband in the latter is allowed an exceptionally romantic escape, reminiscent of the apocalyptic rescue and dance at the end of *The Crock of Gold.* The elaboration of domestic detail is presented only to be mocked and defeated :

'Be back before three o'clock,' said the good lady, 'for the Fegans are coming to tea. You need not take your umbrella, it won't rain and you ought to leave your pipe behind, it doesn't look nice. Bring some cigarettes instead, and your walking-stick if you like, and be sure to be back before three.'

He pressed his pipe into a thing on the wall which was meant for pipes, put his cigarette-case into his pocket, and took his walking-stick in his hand.

The sight of a horse standing patiently in the street sets the docile husband thinking about the way in which society has trapped and cowed humanity into a sort of willing death. He is close to the railway station. In obedience to an unrestrainable impulse he rushes up the steps and takes a train:

> The train gathered speed, went flying out of the station into the blazing sunlight, picked up its heels and ran, and ran, and ran—the wind leaped by the carriage window, shrieking with laughter—the wide fields danced with each other, shouting aloud—
>
> 'The horses are coming again to the green meadows. Make way for the great wild horses!'
>
> And the trees went leaping from horizon to horizon shrieking and shrieking the news.

The passage coming as it does embarrasses criticism for several reasons, the headlong breathlessness, the manic upbeat.[6] And, of course, we know that a train by its nature cannot transport a man beyond society; the husband will not end up in Arcadia but in Limerick Junction, and probably will have to ring his wife for the fare home. But the basic cause of unease stems from the author's fundamental unease with the limits of the realist short story itself. The fabulist finds it difficult to accept the social system as something to be explored and described rather than something to be changed or transcended. The wild plunge of the husband in 'The Horses' could almost be taken as symbolic of the plunge which Stephens will take beyond the conventions of social realism when in his next volume he writes 'Desire' and 'Etched in Moonlight'. Just as the very specially motivated exertion that goes into 'Hunger' respects the idiom and milieu of social realism, and by doing so distils a story that frequently approaches the simplicity of parable.

Fable and Nightmare

The story with which *Etched in Moonlight* opens is entitled 'Desire'. It is a brilliant story, the author's last word on the theme of domestic love, which he now confronts in terms of dream and symbol. On his way home from work a man saves a pedestrian's life and in return is offered one wish which will be fulfilled. After some thought he chooses to remain at his present age, forty-eight years, until he dies. When he tells the story to his wife she is unexpectedly angry:

> 'It is not fair to me,' she explained. 'You are older than I am now, but in a few years this will mean that I shall be needlessly older than you. I think it was not a loyal wish.'
> 'I thought of that objection,' said he, 'and I also thought that I was past the age at which certain things matter; and that both temperamentally and in the matter of years I am proof against sensual or such-like attractions. It seemed to me to be right; so I just registered my wish with him.'[7]

The quarrel does not develop; they laugh at the absurdity of it all and go to bed.

The wife has a dream. She is on a ship in Arctic waters. She is feeling the cold because she has neglected to put on heavy clothes. The ship becomes ice-bound, the crew and passengers get onto the ice. A seaman runs in front of her waving the bundle of her Arctic clothing; everyone abandons her. She wakes up still feeling the cold and snuggles close to her husband in the bed. '... she found that an atrocity of cold came from him; that he was icy. ... He was stone dead. He was stone cold and she stood by him, shivering and whimpering.' Clearly there are many sides to the story. Birgit Bramsbäck stresses symbol and allegory. Like Joyce, she points out, Stephens uses snow to symbolise death. The ship, she argues, 'is the Vehicle of Death, and the captain of the ship is Death himself'.[8] It is also possible to put the emphasis on the ironic outcome of the husband's choice. Like a hundred folk predecessors he is allowed a wish and has it fulfilled to the letter and to his cost. He has tried to hold off Death but has only succeeded, like the servant in the Oriental story, in making an appointment with him at Samarrah.

Yet perhaps it is best seen as a story of the erosion of domestic love. In making his wish the husband leaves his wife out of account. In the realist idiom of the story before the nightmare supervenes, the wife's momentary dismay is real, and stated. Only by adverting to the fact that it is all tomfoolery can she

recover her good humour and go sensibly to bed. In sleep the
reality of her husband's indifference takes shape in dream symbolism. The symbols, especially at first, are not of death but of
cold, loneliness, exclusion, abandonment. In the dream her marriage predicament is piercingly realised—her isolation within a
marriage emptied of love, and therefore of life. By instinct and
habit she turns to her husband for comfort and finds that 'an
atrocity of cold' issues from him.

His bodily death, the petrifaction which in effect he chose,
is emblematic of a prior death of the heart. Yet Stephens is at
pains to insist that they are both sensible, courteous, very normal
people. The fable with its folk pattern, its archetypal symbolism,
its sense of a moral judgment, seems intended to be the story of
Everyman in his domestic predicament. It is certainly one of his
bleakest and most powerful—as well as being one of his final—
comments on conjugal love and its dark alternatives.

The other more realist stories in the volume, 'Schoolfellows',
'Darling', 'The Brute' and 'The Boss' are not as powerful, but
they have in common the theme that energises so many of his
fictions, the problem of communication between man and
woman, man and man. The glass of his vision has darkened.
The interpersonal dialogue, with few exceptions, has become one
of acrimony, misunderstanding, estrangement; the humour which
so often relieved the gloom of his early volume barely flickers in
the later; the only alternative to conflict is a defeated and devas-
tated silence. At the end of 'Schoolfellows' the hero turns in
nausea from a school companion, a parasite who has come to
poison his existence. The loutish unloved man in 'The Wolf' ends
sleeping in the mud having frightened two children with his
clumsy overtures of friendship. The pathetic hero of 'Darling'
loses his job, his wife, his home, his last few pence, and ends
pacing the street and 'thinking that maybe he would see God
through his spectacles'. All are harrowing pictures of unaccom-
modated man and all of them harmonise with the bleak mood of
'Desire'.

The story in *Etched in Moonlight* which most invites comparison with 'Desire' is the long title story. It too can be seen as the
final distillation of a theme that has obsessed Stephens throughout his life, and which has received especial attention in his
fiction, the theme of sexual jealousy. It is a concern which in his

early fiction he took up lightly enough with the policeman's animus against the young clerk in *The Charwoman's Daughter*, Pan's sadness at the loss of Caitilin to Angus Og in *The Crock of Gold*, or in such early short stories as 'The Triangle', 'Three Heavy Husbands', 'Three Lovers Who Lost'. In the case of Patsy MacCann in *The Demi-Gods* it reaches a temporary resolution, but it comes back with absolute ferocity in the obsession of the High King in *Deirdre*. There it is seen as morally destructive; and because Conachur is a King its destructiveness is overwhelming. Stephens might have let the theme rest there, but clearly he was not content to leave the last word on jealousy with his villains. His next treatment of the theme, therefore, is in the story of Eochaidh in 'The Feast of Lugnasa',[9] where he portrays a good man vainly committed in jealousy against god-like power in the person of Midir. Finally, in 'Etched in Moonlight' he dramatises the passion in the person of a man with whom the universal reader can identify; a man, one suspects, very close to the character of Stephens himself. Once the central story gets under way the telling is in the first person; the reader is drawn into the consciousness of the hero, caught up in the momentum of his obsession. The jealous man is now neither villain nor scapegoat; again, as in 'Desire', he tends to be Every-man. Like 'Desire' also, the story has much in common with the medieval morality : the protagonist sins definably and is punished with formal and elaborate justice. Within the dream there are at least two allegorical devices : the purgatorial dungeon and the palpable transformation of the sinner's face in the final sentences. To this may be added the fact that the three characters within the story are embodied principles : the hero stands for possessive and wilful jealousy, his rival for a sort of majestic and invulnerable goodness, the woman for virtue and graciousness. Here Stephens's persistent tendency to strip character at the command of theme reaches a new level of deliberation.

　　The narrator unfolds his dream. He finds himself, at some indeterminate time and place in history, riding along a road towards a castle. He is expected there, and he is led into the presence of the lady he has come to see. He is on fire with impatience for her consent to marry him. She receives him calmly and after eating they go walking with his friend and rival. In the course of the walk he is told that his friend is to marry his beloved. They come to an ancient keep and go in. The lovers enter a dark chamber and the hero slams the door on them. He hurries back to the castle and takes horse for foreign lands. As years pass his sense of guilt grows, though not in the direction of remorse or repentance. Eventually he goes back, only to find that they are alive and happy; they welcome him and soon he is back on the old footing of friendship with them again. In time a marriage is arranged for him. On the night before the wedding the three walk again towards the keep, and as they go he begins to sense a nemesis at work : 'I looked at them; at those faces cut by the moon to a sternness of stone; and I knew in a flash that I was not going between friends but between guards—and that their intention towards me was pitiless.'[10] They impel him to the dungeon and close the door on him. Then follows a period of extreme suffering and fear where he cringes in the darkness. His predicament is vividly reminiscent of that which Poe created for his hero in 'The Pit and the Pendulum' but with Stephens's story there are extra dimensions of guilt and metaphysical dread. His hero tries, for instance, to think of God, but '. . . it seemed to me that God was the blankness behind, which might advance. And that nothing was so awful as the thought of Him—unimaginable and real !' After what seems an interminable wait his companions come and laughingly release him. They explain that they had only been playing with him. On the way back they joke about their own incarceration, explaining that the door had been closed but not locked. The weight of guilt begins to lift from his mind. He feels that at last he has found 'Happiness' ! Then as they reach the castle door the ghastly transformation takes place : 'I saw myself. My mouth was twisted sidewards in a jolly grin. My eyes were turned inwards in a comical squint, and chin was all a sop of my own saliva. I looked at myself so for a mortal moment, and I awakened.'

The deformity is as real as any other incident in the dream. It is not subjective; the others see it too—the lady is horrified by the sight of it. One concludes, therefore, that she and her husband are not numinous presences. They are not the retributive God whom he cringed from in the darkness. What therefore is the relation between the crime and the punishment, the sinner and the nemesis, the hero and his antagonists?

The answer resides in the concept of will which is given

peculiar stress from the outset. As the hero rides towards the castle for the first time, his mind 'full of disquietude, impatience, anger' his will has taken over from all other faculties. He has willed that she shall have him and 'when the will has been invoked ... the mind ... may go on holiday. ... My will was set on that determination'. Not only is it will without reason, but in contrast to the case of Conachur or even the Policeman, it is will without adequate power. His rival has a calm sense of power that he cannot even ruffle, but his will refuses to accept defeat. It leads him to act murderously towards both his rival and his beloved. It denies him the power to repent. He has two opportunities to do so. When he returns and is greeted as a friend, instead of confessing his evil intentions against them he finds himself resenting their goodness: 'My egotism envied them. My shame, and, from it my resentment, was too recent to be laid, though the eyes of a dove looked into mine and the friendliest hand was on my shoulder.' His second opportunity to confess and repent is given him by the purgatorial period in the dungeon. When he is released he accepts their explanation, that they had only been playing with him. He even, as we have seen, fancies that happiness is now available to him. Clearly it is not. He has been, like Gertrude, suppressing his guilt, ignoring it, content to 'skin and film the ulcerous place', while meantime his jealous monomania has been 'mining all within'. Thus, in the climax of the fable the moral evil becomes physical, and to that extent, we may assume, irreversible. God, Stephens seems to be asserting in this extended *exemplum*, is not mocked.

It is not the formal structure or the moral rhetoric that makes 'Etched in Moonlight' a distinguished, if not a great, story but the extraordinary power with which it creates a world. Through the mind of the hero is projected a landscape that vibrates with moral significance. Just as *The Crock of Gold* gives off an aura of sunshine in harmony with the mood of magic and fertility, 'Etched in Moonlight' is the projection of a world apprehended with the intensity and the blindness of obsession. The climate is grey, laced with cool, steely moonlight. The details on which the hero focuses are seen clearly and steadily: the surrounding air is grey, shadowy and sinister, reflecting the nihilism of that area of his consciousness that is not his jealous will:

We reached the extreme of the park. Beyond was a rugged, moon-dozed tumble of earth and bush and rock—and beyond again was the vast silver-straining keep, to which years long gone we three had walked—and from which, and in what agony, I once had fled.

The chill serenity of the scene is in telling contrast to the hero's mounting agitation as he approaches it between his 'guards'. The blackness inside becomes animate—'Darkness that could move, silences that could touch. . . .' When he is released the atmosphere has again adjusted itself to reflect his psychological predicament: 'Our faces were visible to each other as dull shapes, and the spaces about us were bathed in that diaphanous darkness through which one looks without seeing, and against which things loom rather than show.' Here is an impression of that penumbra of moral uncertainty in which the mind of the hero gropes before he opts for his fraudulent version of happiness. Thus the language manages to conjure at once mental states and moral distinctions in a story where phrase, image and narrative rhythm cohere to realise a world where clarity and phantasmagoria press meaning from each other. Indeed, taking into account the large variety of effect that Stephens achieves with prose in a remarkable variety of fiction, nowhere else has he used language with such mastery as in this odd nightmare of the moral imagination.

The Fabulist as Social Critic

Though Stephens repeatedly attacks the theme of social injustice he rarely makes his criticism a strictly Irish concern. His adversary account of the social structure might equally apply to conditions anywhere else in the contemporary urban world. His first prose treatment of the theme is in the interpolated prisoners' stories in *The Crock of Gold* where the relation between worker and employer is seen as humiliating and the power of money oppressive. These themes are treated less seriously in the last cameo of 'Three Lovers Who Lost' where a young clerk who falls in love with his boss's daughter is defeated when the employer uses the professional relationship to separate the lovers. The story of Billy the Music in *The Demi-Gods* exhibits the power of money to brutalise its possessor so that he inevitably brutalises those beneath him. Early poems like 'The Dancer', 'Fifty Pounds a Year, and a Pension', and 'To the Four Courts, Please' are other contributions to the theme. In 'The Boss', the last story of *Etched in Moonlight,* the theme recurs, this time to receive a benign resolution. One of his greatest stories, however, deals with the worker in contemporary society in a manner that relates directly to Dublin social reality and at the same time achieves a universal resonance.

'Hunger' appeared first in booklet form under the pseudonym 'James Esse' in 1918[11] when the defeat of Larkin and his workers in the great lock-out of 1913 was still a bitter memory for many Dubliners. Stephens had written a most violent letter against the clergy and the employers from his Paris exile for *The Irish Worker* five years previously.[12] 'Hunger', though altogether free from polemics, could be seen as an artistic version of his protest against the inhumanity of the social system. It is the closest he gets to *engagé* literature; normally the reformer and the artist in him are separated.

The scene is Dublin and the time is 1914, the aftermath of the lock-out—though that is never mentioned—and the eve of the Great War. A house painter lives in a room with his wife and three children, one of whom is confined to a chair because of a back injury. They are a happy family, united against the impersonal enmity of hunger: 'She had not known for years what it was like not to be hungry for one day—but life is largely custom—and neither she nor her husband nor the children made much complaint about a condition which was normal for them all, and into which the children had been born.'[13] This is the characteristic tone of the story—quiet, matter-of-fact, un-coloured. Rarely does the writer employ imagery, and when he does it is in terms of rudimentary simile, the kind used in conversation. The slow destruction of the family through hunger is conveyed by the quiet and relentless accumulation of bare facts, consecutively recorded.

At best the husband's work is uncertain, good in summer, slack in winter. While things stay normal they manage. Then he is laid up for three weeks with a poisoned hand and their winter savings dwindle. The war comes and he is chronically unemployed. The effect is registered in passages like this:

Almost he had given up looking for work. He would go out of the house and come into the house and go out of the house again; and he and she would look at each other in a dumb questioning.

It was strange how he had arranged with himself not to look at the children. He had even arranged that their whimperings should seem to be inaudible, and their very presences invisible! And they, having raked his coming with search-lights, and discovering that he brought nothing, looked at him no more. They looked at her. They projected themselves to her, about her, into her . . .

The sense of helplessness, of numb despair is caught in the muted undertone of the prose, the dull factual cadences, the details of gesture and evasion by which husband, wife and children are cowed in the palpable presence of the enemy. The narrating voice goes on implacably recording events. The youngest child dies 'of an ill which, whatever it was at the top, was hunger at the bottom'. The husband hears of work in a munitions factory in Scotland and the money is found to pay his passage there. They must starve till he sends them money:

'Write, if you can', she said, 'the minute you get a place.'
'Yes,' he replied.
'And send us what you can spare,' she said. 'Send something this week if you can.'
'Yes,' he said.
And he went away.
And she went into the streets to beg.

The repeated monosyllables—'if you can', 'yes', 'and'—and the weary rhythm of their fall, suggest hope on the brink of exhaustion.

They foreshadow a week in which the family manages to cling to life, but which brings no news from Scotland. The mother manages to get help from a charitable organisation and comes home to find her second child dead of hunger. The next evening a gentleman from a charitable organisation comes to see her: '. . . to a room swept almost as clean as a dog kennel is, to the staring wise-eyed child who lived in a chair; and to the quiet morsel of death that lay on a cot by the wall.' The rude simplicity of the simile, the stillness and desperate passivity in the adjectives, again the implacable rhythm of the monosyllables, carry the central emotion which is the story's theme. The facts of the husband's fate are simply recorded. He had got work in the factory a fortnight after he had applied and on the following morning he had been found in a lane, dead of exposure and malnutrition.

The story exhibits above all Stephens's remarkable instinct for narrative style. It would be hard to find a more vivid stylistic contrast than that provided between 'Hunger' and 'Etched in Moonlight', the one monosyllabic, concrete, quotidian, the other elaborate, imagistic, remote. Yet both are stories of essences, both embody clearly articulated themes through simple agents, a world of 'he' and 'she' and 'they'. The endemic thrift with which he handles theme and character serves the intensity of his vision equally in both stories, a fact which is deftly registered by Lloyd Frankenberg when he remarks of 'Hunger' that 'Only a master of fantasy could have distilled such a nightmare of fact.'[14]

5

The Demi-Gods

The Grand Design

 The Demi-Gods is, up to this point, Stephens's most ambitious fiction as well as being his most intricate experiment in narrational strategy. While essentially a comic fantasy it has, like *The Crock of Gold*, a serious prophetic dimension; and it goes beyond its predecessor in taking the action back to the creation of the world and into the heavens, Christian, Kabbalistic and Theosophical. Its central theme is the war of the sexes, and this conflict is not only dramatised in the earthly and the celestial arenas, but is shown to be the same struggle proceeding on two separate and related planes. In the service of this Miltonic ambition Stephens deploys the elaborate narrative method that makes the book such a curious technical achievement.

 The fable begins with the tinkers, Patsy MacCann and his daughter, Mary, pitching camp for the evening on the roadside of Knockbeg. Here they are joined by three angels, Finaun, Caeltia and Art. The MacCanns agree to adopt the angels as part of their company; the celestial garments are hidden and replaced by clothes which Patsy steals for the occasion, and the remaining chapters of Book I describe their wanderings round the roads of Ireland and their encounters with other vagrants of their kind.

 Book II, 'Eileen Ni Cooley', describes their meeting with a tinker woman of that name, a woman with whom Patsy has a relationship which swings violently between love and antagonism. As the company shelters in a deserted house the two quarrel, fight and are reconciled. It is here, in Chapter XVI, that the first radical shift in the narrative takes place. Finaun, the eldest angel, who bears a striking resemblance to Eileen, recounts his story of creation : In the beginning there had been two creatures

called Finaun and Caeltia Mac Dea (the surname being the Irish
for 'son of god'), male and female principles whose sexes constantly interchanged, destined to 'pursue each other with a hate
which is slowly changing to love'. We realise by this time that
each of the angels has an earthly counterpart—the word must
serve for the moment—among the tinkers: Finaun, the Archangel,
is paired with Eileen; Caeltia, the Seraph, with Patsy; and Art,
the Cherub, with Mary. In another relation Finaun has a special
affinity with the ass, who turns out to be in some senses the most
sagacious and contemplative of the party, and this affinity is
shared by Mary. As Finaun tells his story Patsy falls asleep, but
when it is ended Caeltia tells him that he has been awake and
listening on Patsy's behalf. Eileen liked the story and understood it, but could not translate its meaning into words. As the
second book ends Eileen, because of Patsy's taunts about her
promiscuity, has stolen away from the company.

In Book III they meet a tramp called Billy the Music. Billy
embarks on a story, his story, in the course of which a most
complex pattern of narratives begin to unfold. Raising a theme
which takes second place to love in the novel, he tells the history
of his former greed when he had been a rich farmer and of his
conversion. The conversion had been brought about by a supernatural visitation : the Seraph Cuchulain accompanied by a certain Brien O'Brien, both recently expelled from the christian
heaven, had come and threatened him with severe punishments if
he failed to mend his ways. Cuchulain had put the case in these
terms :

> 'I'm your Higher Self,' said he, 'and every rotten business you
> do down here does be vibrating against me up there. . . .
> You're a miser and a thief, and you got me thrown out of
> heaven because of the way you loved money. . . . You made a
> thief of me in a place where it's no fun to be a robber, and
> here I am wandering the dirty world on the head of your
> unrighteous ways.'

At the mention of Cuchulain and O'Brien Patsy is galvanised
into furious attention and insists on interpolating a story of his
own concerning them into Billy the Music's narrative. Patsy's story
relates how Cuchulain and O'Brien, on naked arrival on earth,
had waylaid the MacCanns on the Donnybrook Road and had

stripped them of their clothes—hence Cuchulain's being dressed as a woman throughout the entire action of the novel.

When Billy's story is finished, Caeltia fills in the extra-terrestrial detail of the Cuchulain-O'Brien saga. In a hilarious narrative he tells how O'Brien had arrived in the next world clutching a threepenny piece, how Cuchulain had found it on the floor of heaven and had refused to hand it over to the judge, Rhadamantus, thus causing the expulsion of both from eternity back to earth. This story is followed in Chapter XXVII by Art's account of a struggle with O'Brien at an earlier stage of his karma, this time in the theosophist heaven and at a crucial stage of the world's evolution. At the end of Book III therefore we have, by means of ingeniously dovetailed narratives, come abreast of the history of all the characters in its earthly and celestial manifestation.

By the second chapter of the fourth and last book, entitled 'Mary MacCann', Eileen Ni Cooley together with O'Brien and Cuchulain, has come again upon the MacCann encampment, this time looking for Patsy's protection from the troglodyte O'Brien, the most recent in her procession of lovers. In the complex of assaults and counter-assaults that follow, the ass kicks O'Brien in the head and dispatches him once again into the intricate pathways of his karma. The book then proceeds, with one complication, to its conclusion, when the two elder angels return to the heavens and the Cherub, Art, remains as Mary's earthly lover. The complication is Patsy's temporary lapse into greed which leads him to steal off in the night and sell the angels' celestial robes, an action which he repents of and repairs before the fable ends.

The narrative scheme is then simple in outline, complex in detail. The over-arching form is that of the romantic comedy: two sets of lovers, Art and Mary, Patsy and Eileen, proceed through a series of misunderstandings and reversals to happy union in the book's last pages. The spirit of the book is predominantly picaresque: the protagonists are all engaging rogues and the action takes the form of apparently aimless journeying and random adventure. In retrospect, as Benedict Kiely shrewdly points out, all the 'little heedless roads that the angels and tinkers travelled together led back to the place where the celestial garments of Caeltia and Finaun and Art had been hidden so that they could for a time appear like men in the world of men.'[1] In consonance with the spirit of 'picaresque' the book is an implicit celebration of the Dionysian principle in man, his tendency towards passion, imagination and excess, and a rejection of the Apollonian values of prudence, reason and social stability. It is one of the book's multiple ironies that the angels, for all their christian style, title and regalia, assent without demur to the tinkers' amoral and predatory code and show no curiosity about the safer values by which the settled community lives. Thus the broad outline of the book's scheme, the comic picaresque, recounts a story wherein angels come down from the heavens and assist earthly lovers in composing their differences, a process that is sealed by one of their number choosing to remain on earth as lover of the tinker's daughter. This over-arching pattern is conveyed mostly in the first and last books of the novel which are both free—with one slight exception—from interpolated or reflexive narrative. The two centre books of the novel with their intricate and complementary story patterns range between earth and heaven and seek, in a spirit of mischievous inquiry, to clarify the ways of god to man.

The Cosmic Comedy

Stephens wrote to Lord Dunsany in 1910 in these terms: 'These three words I think best criticise your work—Spontaneity —movement—zest—the zest is enormous. Do you know that your prose work—that is the basic feeling in it & my later verse are curiously alike—we are seeing the same thing, great windy reaches, & wild flights among the stars & a very youthful laughter at the gods.'[2] And in the following year he added: 'I only know of one morality—and that is Energy. I call every *thing* or *thought* that acquiesces or sits down Vice & I call everything that disobeys, & refuses, & breaks, "Virtue" & again I call Force Virtue & Energy Vice and the latter seems to me the better of the two. ...A city would travel as long a distance on Blasphemy & Laughter as on Prayer & Fasting & be much better to live in.'[3]

The poems he is referring to are those like 'MacDhoul' which involve wild flights and youthful laughter at the gods, and it is likely that Stephens's reading of Dunsany's prose fantasies opened to him the possibility of exploring the heavens in that spirit of laughter and blasphemy that he finds congenial to his inspiration. His remarks, however, are useful in another direction. They provide a salutary warning to the critic who is tempted to approach a work like *The Demi-Gods* expecting to find in it a systematic application of any single doctrine, Theosophical, Biblical, Blakean or Kabbalist. Elements of all are unquestionably present but they are present in a combination that answers only to the demands of the author's artistic conscience. And even when, as in Finaun's tale of creation, a doctrine is presented in direct and extended form, it is always modified by its context in the book's dynamism.

The angels are dressed in the traditional accoutrement of angels as presented by artists and writers of the christian church —wings, robes, adornments of gold and silver. But their mission is scandalously untraditional: they make no effort to influence MacCann against stealing and getting drunk, and are happy to enjoy the fruits of his tireless pillage. Seen in the light of Blakean doctrine they might fit his theory of 'emanations': Finaun and Art could be seen as coming on earth to join their female counterparts, Eileen and Mary respectively. But the theory breaks down if applied to Caeltia and Patsy, both of whom are aggressively male, whereas the 'Emanation' in Blake's system is necessarily female. Consequently it is clear that while Stephens is drawing on Blake he is doing so in the spirit of ruthless eclecticism.

The story of Brien O'Brien and his threepenny piece is especially revealing. In the Irish folk equivalents to this story the sinner is brought before St Peter at the gates of heaven, a convention exploited by Yeats in 'The Fiddler of Dooney'. Stephens retains the traditional décor of the Christian heaven, but instead of Peter he has Rhadamantus—whom Greek legend had consigned as a judge to the infernal regions—guarding the gate and dispensing justice among the blessed. Among the Seraphs he has Cuchulain, one of the most bloodthirsty heroes from the world of Celtic paganism. And when Rhadamantus throws him and O'Brien out of heaven there is a sustained parodic echo of Milton as they are seen falling giddily past 'Chaos and empty Nox'.

The two descriptions of creations given by Finaun and Art derive frankly from *The Secret Doctrine*, specifically from Madame Blavatsky's quotation from the Book of Dyzan where the role of 'The Army of the Voice' and of the 'Seven Sons of Creation' is set out :

> There was the Army of the Voice, the Divine Mother of the Seven. The Sparks of the Seven are subject to, and the servants of, the first, the second, the third, the fourth, the fifth, the sixth and the seventh of the seven. These (Sparks) are called spheres, triangles, cubes, lines and modellers : for thus stands the eternal Nidana—Oi-Ha-Hou. (i.e. 'the ceaseless and eternal Cosmic Motion, or rather Force, that moves it, which Force is tacitly accepted as the Deity, but never named. It is the eternal Karana, the ever-acting Cause'.)[4]

Finaun's account of the first phase of creation concentrates on the struggle between himself and Caeltia, the aboriginal male and female principles, through a succession of ages. Both have the second name of Mac Dea, son of god, and are therefore children of the 'eternal Cosmic Motion'. They are alternately male and female 'that their battle might be joined in the intimacy which can only come through difference and the distance that is attraction.' As they struggle through succeeding cycles of existence their enmity begets a series of abstract values such as 'knowledge, the parent of love', 'contempt', 'cunning', 'repugnance', 'affection'. Out of the conflict is born a demon, 'the accumulation of their evil'. The demon, now seen successively as the spirit of 'Misery' and the 'Spectre', makes the woman his concubine, giving her energy and knowledge. The woman uses the Spectre, Misery, as her emissary to the male. He leaps upon the demon and is carried with him into the pit of hell which their enmity had created.

This account of the world's first phase is not especially coherent, nor does the reader of the novel tend to linger long to extract doctrinal wisdom from it. He knows that a cosmic version of the Fall is being recounted, a supra-natural history of the division of the sexes and their eternal effort towards re-integration. The love-hate relationship between Patsy and Eileen, and their attendant celestial counterparts—Finaun and Caeltia—is thereby given an archetypal resonance which lends an expectancy above the merely natural to the drama of their attraction and enmity as tinkers on the roads of Ireland. The reader also senses that this drama has an ancient counterpart in the story of Eden where the demon entered to place the seed of knowledge in the mind of the female. And if he is a student of Blake he knows that the Spectre is man's enemy:

> Each man is in his Spectre's power,
> Until the arrival of that hour
> When his Humanity awake
> And cast the Spectre into the lake.[5]

But no laborious annotation of the interpolated story from any of its obvious sources will extend its relevance for the novel, nor is any specialist knowledge of these sources necessary for an appreciation of the story and its role within the many-layered intricacy of Stephens's fable. Each component story is a gloss, an illumination and a criticism of its fellows.

The point is more clearly evident in Art's description of the later phase of the world's emanation in Chapter XXVII, towards the end of Book III. Here Art—identifiable as one of the 'seven sons' of the first 'Primordial Seven' in Blavatsky's doctrine[6]—labours with 'The Army of the Voice' to produce a new movement in the world's emanation. As he waits for the 'second syllable' of the Voice he finds himself hindered by Brien O'Brien. O'Brien at this stage of his karma is a being of the fifth round, one round above the level of earthly existence.[7] O'Brien announces himself as 'a great magician . . . and a great humorist', and under these auspices he determines to perpetrate a joke against Art and against the purposes of the creating deity. He has surrounded himself with a protective shield of kabbalistic triangles which prevent Art from destroying him. But his magical calculations go astray and the tables are turned on him. He is punished by having to forfeit his evolution and by having his karmic burden trebled. He is driven back to earth as a mere man; only one of O'Brien's interstellar mishaps. He is the cosmic buffoon of the novel as he shuttles between one state of being and the next, punished equally for his inordinate love of money and his doomed pretensions as an occult humorist. ' "No magician has a sense of humour," remarked Finaun, "he could not be a magician if he had—Humour is the health of the mind." '

This last instance of Stephens's eclecticism in his handling of esoteric doctrine is the surest indication of its role in the comic structure of the novel. There has been a recurrent note of parody in the idiom of *The Crock of Gold* where the theories of Yeats and Russell and the styles of Synge and Colum were casually parodied. Here the opposition of the Theosophists and the Kabbalists is gently satirised. In a penetrating master's thesis on the subject Miss Lorraine Weir goes so far as to suggest that the entire *Demi-Gods* can be read as an erudite mockery of the controversies of Yeats, Blavatsky, Mathers and AE : 'For indulging in magical conjuration of precisely the sort O'Brien uses here, Yeats was dismissed from the (Hermetic) Society. The psychic duel between Art and Brien is then a send-up of the *fin-de-siècle* rivalry between the theosophists and the Kabbalists, a burlesque of "Dublin's gods and half-gods".'[8] Pushing her theory of parody to its full extension Miss Weir goes on to suggest that the contemplative donkey in the novel is an affectionate portrait of the mystical AE. It is not necessary to go so far in parodic exegesis to recognise the validity of her view that much of the doctrinal drama of *The Demi-Gods* is not very solemnly intended. That it is offered by a comic writer in the spirit of 'very youthful laughter at the gods'.

The cosmic comedy extends down and up along the great chain of being. The book opens with MacCann's impatient rebuke to Mary for her habit of kissing the donkey. She insists that the ass likes it :

> 'That's not a reason; sure it doesn't matter in the world what an ass likes or dislikes, and, anyhow, an ass doesn't like anything except carrots and turnips.'
> 'This one does,' said she stoutly.
> 'And a body might be kissing an ass until the black day of doom and he wouldn't mind it.'
> 'This one minds.'
> 'Kissing an old ass !'
> 'One has to be kissing something.'

Clearly MacCann has a great deal more than Mary to learn about the universe before he is ready for the mystery of love and knowledge which he enters upon at the end.

Through the fable animals, birds, insects and vegetation are endowed with different degrees of psychic life and energy. In Chapter VI the ass wakes first and the 'very sun itself leaped across the horizon and stared at him with its wild eye'. The donkey's eye is 'hazy with cogitation'. A crow perches delightedly on a hedge : 'he polished his feet with his bill, and then polished his bill on his left thigh, and then he polished his left thigh with the back of his neck. "I'm a hell of a crow," said he, "and everybody admits it." ' When, in Chapter XVIII, they shelter in the deserted house, Art, himself a scholar of reincarnation, has the following colloquy with a spider :

'Are the times bad with you now, or are they middling?'

'Not so bad, glory be to God ! The flies do wander through the holes, and when they come from the light outside to the darkness in here, sir, we catch them on the wall, and we crunch their bones.'

'Do they like that?'

'They do not, sir, but we do. The lad with the stout, hairy legs, down there beside your elbow, caught a blue-bottle yesterday; there was eating on that fellow I tell you, and he's not all eaten yet, but that spider is always lucky, barring the day he caught a wasp.'

'That was a thing he didn't like?'

'Don't mention it to him, sir, he doesn't care to talk about it.'

'What way are you going to fasten up your rope?' said Art.

'I'll put a spit on the end of it, and then I'll thump it with my head to make it stick.'

'Well, good luck to yourself.'

'Good luck to your honour.'

Moments like this in *The Demi-Gods* are too often dismissed as mere Stephensian whimsy, capricious displays of drollery, amusing in themselves but unrelated to the book's main action. Only when we take account of the book's larger design, its impudently cosmic scope, does their place in its comic strategy become clear.

The Comedy of Love

The related stories of Patsy and Mary MacCann and their relationships with Eileen and Art—and by extension with Finaun and Caeltia—are primarily concerned with the theme of love, secondarily with the theme of money. The stories of Billy the Music, of O'Brien and Cuchulain, are exclusively concerned with money in its earthly and eternal implication.

Throughout the novel the attitudes of Patsy and Mary to-

wards the angels are sharply distinguished. MacCann, having
first welcomed the visitors, proposes that he and his daughter
steal away in the early morning. His response is at once more
cautious and conventional than his daughter's—' "we don't know
who them fellows are at all, and what would the priest say if he
heard we were stravaiging the country with three big, buck
angels, and they full of tricks maybe?" ' Mary, who has already
begun to fall in love with Art, and whose womanly compassion is
stirred by the plight of their disoriented visitants, only succeeds
in changing Patsy's mind by pointing out the angels' gold rings
and other signs of their wealth. Patsy is persuaded but his predatory instinct lies dormant for most of the action until his greed
comes perilously to the surface again in the closing chapters of
the novel. His acquiescence is buttressed by a second, more
archetypal instinct and motive:

> In his soul the Ancient Patriarch was alive and ambitious for
> leadership. Had his wife given him more children he would
> have formed them and their wives and children into a band,
> and the affairs of this little world would have been directed
> by him with pride and pleasure . . . he would have taken to the
> road, like a prince of old, with his tail, and he would have
> undertaken such raids and forays that his name and fame
> would ring through the underworld like the note of a trumpet.

When he gives himself to this role he discharges it with a touch-
ing and elaborate courtesy. Stephens's skill with narrative and
dialogue is finely evident in a passage like this where the angels
ask their host to show them how to go about eating:

> 'I'll stand in nobody's light, and teaching people is God's
> own work; this is the way I do it, your worships, and any one
> that likes can follow me up.'
> He seized two pieces of bread, placed a slice of cheese
> between them, and bit deeply into that trinity.
> The strangers followed his actions with fidelity, and in a
> moment their mouths were as full as his was and as content.
> 'When I've this one finished,' said he, 'I'll put a lump of
> meat between them, and I'll eat that.'
> 'Ah!' said one of the angels whose mouth chanced to be
> free.
> Patsy's eye roved over the rest of the food.

'And after that,' he continued, 'we will take a bit of what-ever is handy.'

There had been nothing quite like this in Irish or indeed in English fiction before. In *The Crock of Gold*, as we have seen, the magical and the numinous become credible in a world that has been from the opening line carefully prepared to receive them. The fictional world of Lewis Carroll is at a radical remove from the quotidian. Even in a later Irish fantasist such as Flann O'Brien—whose debt to Stephens is demonstrable—the blend of the fabulous and the realistic works in deliberate and absurd counterpoint. But here, without apparent strain, the angels and the tinkers are subsumed into a fictional pattern of shared and credible dialogue; the numinous and the miraculous are tamed and domesticated.

When the company sights Eileen Ni Cooley with her sham-bling lover on the road before them an exchange between Patsy and his counterpart, Caeltia, introduces Stephens's theme of sexual antinomies:

'Do you not like that woman?' Caeltia enquired.
'She's a bad woman,' replied Patsy.
'What sort of bad woman is she?'
'She's the sort that commits adultery with every kind of man,' he said harshly.
'Did she ever commit adultery with yourself?'
'She did not,' said Patsy, 'and that's why I don't like her.'
Caeltia considered that statement also, and found it reason-able:
'I think,' said he, 'that the reason you don't like that woman is because you like her too much.'

Further in the exchange he suggests to Patsy—' "that the reason you don't want to see her is because you want to see her too much".' Patsy grumpily assents to both propositions. His rival and his opposite in the rhetoric of love, the gangling tramp, is vividly caught in one of Stephens's more memorable brief character sketches: 'Nothing of comeliness remained to him but his eyes, which were timid and tender as those of a fawn, and his hands which had never done anything but fumble with women.' In sharp contrast to Patsy he senses that Eileen no longer desires his company and immediately goes, leaving the field to MacCann.

When the company assemble in the deserted house Patsy misses his chance of winning Eileen by falling asleep for Finaun's story which would have given him the clue to the cosmic opposition at work between himself and Eileen. In the dialogue of love he is the last to learn; it falls to Eileen, who has heard and understood the story, to take the initiatives which bring them finally together.

The impediment to Patsy's sexual and spiritual enlightenment is his single-minded and relentless pursuit of sustenance, which in its more sinister manifestation becomes a pursuit of possessions. In the last book of the novel, succumbing to greed he steals and sells the angels' garments. When in Chapter XXXI he is persuaded to recover them, 'a tempered happiness radiated [from him] as of old' and he can look at his daughter 'with the cynical kindliness habitual to him'. His reconciliation with Eileen Ni Cooley is triggered by his observation of the married couple at whose house he had sold the garments. This curious interpolation in which the husband reproaches his unfaithful wife with her adulteries and receives nothing in return but cold contempt would be hard to account for in other terms. In it MacCann sees, however unconsciously, the folly of his jealousy at Eileen Ni Cooley's relentless infidelities. And when Caeltia persuades him to throw away the money he had received in his treacherous escapade, the way is open for their love to develop unforced : ' "Stick your arm through mine, Eileen," said he, "and let us be comfortable as we go along, for the pair of us haven't had a talk for a long time, and Caeltia here wants to talk to you as well as me." '

Mary's characterisation is not nearly so sharp, dramatic or individualised as MacCann's, and her love affair with Art develops in the novel only by hint and indirection. Their relationship would in fact appear as a parody of youthful, romantic love if it were not for its thematic centrality to the novel's action. Until the end they exchange not a word of conversation; their mutual attraction is conveyed in a series of bashful glances and oblique acknowledgments, in Mary's favouritism towards the young angel in the dispensation of food, her reluctance to be alone with him, her inability to engage him in conversation. His celestial background unfits him for the role of lover so that he can only express himself in athletic gestures on the walls and ditches and in snatches of half-learnt ballads. His name is probably significant; when he tears up his wings at the end he seems destined to support himself and his bride as an itinerant ballad singer and musician.

Thematically their union echoes that of Caitilin and Angus Og at the conclusion of *The Crock of Gold*. It is a marriage of the human and the divine. The mission of Caeltia and Finaun is complete once they have brought into equilibrium the cosmic opposition of Patsy and Caeltia, their earthly counterparts. The union of the younger generation, as is traditional in the comic romance, sets the seal of reconciliation on the divisions of the older. A new era of harmony between the sexes is thereby initiated. Thus the last words of Art echo those of Angus Og: ' "Let you and I go down after the people," he said. But Mary was weeping, and as they paced down the narrow track he laid a great arm about her shoulders.'

The Comedy of Greed

When Patsy MacCann obeys his guardian angel Caeltia and throws his ill-gotten wealth away he lets one piece of gold slip through his fingers into the bottom of his pocket. Before parting from Caeltia he confesses to the deception. Caeltia permits him to keep it. ' "I'll keep it," said he earnestly, "and I'll spend it." ' The occasion marks a return to his proper code of day-to-day survival. This code has been scrupulously defined in Chapters IX and X of the novel where the issues of property rights and the organisation of capitalist society are analysed with a deceptive casualness. In Chapter IX Patsy is described as a man who stood so far 'outside of every social relation' that 'within an organised humanity he might almost have been reckoned as a different species'. Social man is defined in terms of two dimensions of mobility: he 'goes up the social scale and down it' and he moves between 'the place where he works and the place where he lives'. It is in the latter dimension that he finds 'all the freedom he can hope for'. MacCann lives only in the horizontal dimension, and here he enjoys the fullness of his liberty. He is as free from social morality as he is from social convention: 'in the immense, neglected pastures of civilisation he found his own quietude and his own wisdom'. Civilisation has 'built itself at hazard upon the Rights of Property' and upon 'the great Ethic of Possession' from

D

which it has tried to escape occasionally but in vain. At two moments in the book MacCann had almost been corrupted by these values, and had thereby placed at risk his peculiar karmic destiny.

In the prisoners' stories in *The Crock of Gold*, in several of the stories that make up *Here Are Ladies* and *Etched in Moonlight*, and in many of the early poems, Stephens saw the relation between worker and employer as almost intrinsically degrading. Thus, in Chapter VIII of *The Demi-Gods* MacCann tells the angels of a subversive itinerant who had outlined to him the capitalist structure in these terms : 'he said that the folk at the top do grab all the food in the world, and that then they make every person work for them, and that when you've done a certain amount of work they give you just enough money to buy just enough food to let you keep on working for them.' Being a hunter himself he has never been attracted by the system. This makes him a useful audience for Billy the Music when the latter recounts his tale of greed, exploitation and conversion in the third book of the novel.

Like the story of the threepenny piece, to which it is related, Billy's story is adapted from a folk tale, in his case that of King Midas. Before his conversion to evangelical vagrancy he had been a rich farmer whose being had become gradually consumed by greed. He had starved his family and exploited his workers and continued to turn his money into gold pieces. These slowly had become his god. His justification had been the rapacity of the capitalist system with which he had had to do business : 'I found that there was a world outside of my world, and it was truly robbing me, and, what's more, it had thought hard for generations about the best way of doing it.' MacCann, who had once stolen from Billy in the latter's days of affluence, assures him that he 'would have broken his teeth with a spade' if he had been one of Billy's workers :

'If you had been one of my men,' the other replied mildly, 'you'd have been as tame as a little kitten; you'd have crawled round me with your hat in your hand and your eyes turned up like a dying duck's, and you'd have said, "Yes, sir", and "No, sir" like the other men that I welted the stuffing out of with my two fists, and broke the spirits of with labour and

hunger. Don't be talking now, for you're an ignorant man in these things, although you did manage to steal a clocking hen off me the day I was busy.'
'And a pair of good boots,' said Patsy triumphantly.

Billy's change of heart comes about in a manner analogous to Patsy's: his greed had 'vibrated' against his guardian angel, Cuchulain, in heaven, so that the latter was sent forcibly to earth where he set about putting things straight. His method was to curse Billy with so much gold that the latter could not count it any more, and took to the roads with his concertina leaving his useless riches behind.

Brien O'Brien's story is related to that of Billy the Music's by the same theme of greed. He had died after a life of meanness. When he was being waked a neighbour had slipped a threepenny piece into his daughter's hand. 'Little Shiela', as Caeltia narrates, 'had been well trained by her father':

she tiptoed to the coffin and slipped the threepenny-piece into Brien's hand. The hand had never refused money when it was alive, it did not reject it either when it was dead.

When O'Brien dropped it on the floor in heaven and Cuchulain picked it up and refused to part with it he was acting under the malign influence of Billy's greed on earth. O'Brien's greed had, if anything, been intensified by his confinement in hell. His uproar there—a variation on another Irish folk motif—had made hell unendurable for its other inhabitants so that Rhadamantus deemed it better for all concerned that he be cast, with Cuchulain, back to earth. It is consistent with the book's logic that the donkey, whose inner life is one of mystical meditation and visionary quiet, finds O'Brien's unruly presence in the camp equally unendurable, and kicks him accurately on the head thus sending him to trouble yet another plane of karmic existence: 'The donkey had again related the infinity without with the eternity within, and his little hoofs were as peaceful as his mild eye.'

Relating the comedy of love to the comedy of greed, we see that the intricate stories of Finaun, Caeltia, Art and Billy provided Patsy MacCann with sufficient *exempla* for a wise man to learn by. But MacCann is not a wise man like Christy Mahon he is 'a poor learner, a middling scholar only'. In his stubborn consciousness the operation of grace makes sluggish progress, and it is only through a painful ordeal of instruction and suffering that he comes to self-knowledge. He is the one complex character in the book, and it is his progress towards redemptive love that gives the book its main energy and coherence. In him the themes of love and money work themselves out and arrive at a final resolution, and the fable reaches a conclusion in which the reader can finally acquiesce.

In choosing the comic form and spirit for his vision in *The Demi-Gods* Stephens was not implying that his theme was slight or merely laughable. The choice of form was deeply related to his view of creation : he needed a narrative morphology and idiom which would enable him to embrace within one fictive structure a vision of the world which would show the interdependence and interrelation of the spiritual with the physical, the terrestrial with the supernatural, the animal and vegetable with the human. *The Demi-Gods* is not a large book, but its scope is Miltonic. It engages, through the agency of laughter, the Christian, the Blakean, the Kabbalistic and the Theosophist accounts of the universe, and manages to combine and compose them within an over-view that is peculiarly his own. It employs a variety of narrative conventions; the realistic idiom of fiction where the reader moves in a world not dissimilar from that of Synge's plays and notebooks; the mock epic with its Byronic comedy of angels; the moral *exemplum* and the Irish folk tale; the picaresque with its apparent aimlessness but underlying design and purpose; the social-realist idiom of domestic disharmony; the animal fable. The varieties of theology and the diversity of literary forms are cunningly fitted together, are made interdependent, so that the multiple layers of reality find expression in the multiple inter-action of narrative morphologies. The complexity of the world-view finds expression in the complexity of the telling, the con-stantly shifting point of view, the ever-changing angle of vision. *The Demi-Gods* is, up to this point, Stephens's most radical experiment with world-within-world, story-within-story. His view of the world and of the fictional enterprise will continue to develop, finding its most elaborate expression in his handling of epic and mythic material in his last extended fiction, *In the Land of Youth*. In *The Demi-Gods* it has achieved a degree of success that is to prove exemplary for later generations of experimental fiction writers.

6

Georgian Pastoral
and Childhood Epiphany

SONGS FROM THE CLAY 1915
THE ADVENTURES OF SEUMAS BEG 1915

The Attrition of Influence

The influence of Blake and Browning on Stephens's early poetry was largely beneficial. Both were daringly original and nonconformist in their religious and social attitudes and therefore provided a healthy example for a poet who was himself subversive in his instincts. Blake's mythic and visionary writings showed Stephens how the imagination could, through poetry and fiction, provide the individual with a symbolic landscape in which his deeper aspirations and convictions might take on autonomous life. For a mind untrained in and hostile to abstract reasoning—see the opening lines of 'The Breath of Life'—this was invaluable as example and inspiration. Browning, on the other hand, had shown Stephens a dramatic technique and a conversational idiom which enabled him to interrogate the world of lived, local experience through the device of scenario and persona. In each case Stephens treated his source selectively, adapting and appropriating what was essential to his own creative purpose. Thus in the prose fantasy, where the process of adaptation was more radical, a more radical originality resulted. Both influences were liberating : Blake and Browning were writers of great amplitude, wide-ranging explorers of time and space. From their example Stephens learned to push out the confines of his local world and attempt the 'great windy reaches and wild flights among the stars' which he admired so much in Dunsany. He was therefore enabled to lay creative hold on the body of Irish mythology already to hand in the work of O'Grady and Lady Gregory, in the doctrines of AE and the Theosophists, and to shape from that material a mythic and visionary system harmonious with his own intuitions and beliefs.

He was not nearly so fortunate when he turned from the visionary, the dramatic and the mythic to the more conventional idiom of nature poetry. Here the influence of the 'precursor' whether remote and massive, like Spenser or Wordsworth, or contemporary and slight, like Hodgson or de la Mare, tended to impose not only the method and the language but also the subject matter itself on the poet's sensibility. The result is that with Stephens his nature poetry from *Insurrections* to *Seumas Beg* is a history of almost progressive deterioration. Every stage can be marked by the intrusion of a new influence insufficiently absorbed or adapted to produce a convincing originality in the resulting verse.

His early experiments in the nature lyric are remarkably promising. 'The Shell' (C.P., p. 27) has achieved a modest celebrity in the anthologies. There are unmistakable Wordsworthian echoes in such lines as 'The slow, sad murmur of far distant seas,' and in the sound of pebbles 'Forever rolling, with a hollow sound,' but the nightmare quality of the experience is the poet's own recognisable contribution :

> It was a sunless strand, that never bore
> The footprint of a man,
> Nor felt the weight
>
> Since time began
> Of any human quality or stir,
> Save what the dreary winds and wave incur.

The diction is still derivative and conventional, but one senses the fantasist's imagination about its proper business. We are reminded of certain desolate images from stories like 'Desire' and 'Etched in Moonlight'. The swing of the rhythm is original and precise as it mimes the movement of the waves in their ebb and flow across the beach :

> And bubbling sea-weeds, as the waters go,
> Swish to and fro
> Their long cold tentacles of slimy grey;

The imagined situation where the speaker presses the shell to his ear at the start and dispels the ensuing phantasm by taking it away at the end

> Oh, it was sweet
> To hear a cart go jolting down the street.

successfully frames the experience.

In *A Poetry Recital* published in 1925 Stephens has a short, experimental poem called 'The Main Deep' (C.P., p. 29). Introducing it he says that his poem is an attempt to convey the 'roll rush and march of great waters'. He complains of Byron's famous apostrophe to the ocean that it gives only two lines to the ocean and the rest to meditations on human ambition and the transcience of life. The first stanza of 'The Main Deep' gives an idea of its method and effectiveness :

> The long-rólling,
> Steady-póuring,
> Deep-trenchéd
> Green billów :

The success is problematical, though Yeats deemed it worth including in his *Oxford Book of Modern Verse*. It does not however provide a clue to what Stephens attempts in these early lyrics and what he attempts in his moments of genuine originality throughout his nature poetry. In these moments he aims at imaginative surrender to the object perceived in order to absorb and express its quiddity, its peculiar essence. The degree of success achieved in 'The Shell' derives from his drawing the reader into the rhythmic life of his imagined sea-scape. The same process gives a feeling of achieved experience to another of his lyrics in *Insurrections* entitled 'The Chill of Eve' (C.P., p. 25) in some of its better stanzas :

> Spread cold and far,
> Without one glow
> From a mild pale star,
> In the sky's steel bow;
> And the grey
> Chill day
> Slips away
> Below.

Again the language is conventionally poetic, but the movement
of the lines—repeated in each of the stanzas—catches the gradual
recession of daylight, the oncoming chill of night in its slow
inevitable process. The poem is resolutely about the evening, not
at all about the poet. Already Stephens senses certain possibilities
in the lyric form which he is to define in his Preface to the
Collected Poems of 1926. There he states that 'the lyrical poet is
undisputed master of all the *extremes* that can be expressed in
terms of speed or tempo', and that 'a swift lyrical line is as
quick as lightning; a slow one can be slower than a snail'.

A lyric entitled 'The Wind' (C.P., p. 116)[1] demonstrates the
theory at the opposite extreme of speed to 'The Chill of Eve':

> The wind stood up, and gave a shout;
> And whistled on his fingers and
>
> Kicked the withered leaves about,
> And thumped the branches with his hand,
>
> And said he'll kill, and kill, and kill;
> And so he will! And so he will!

The impression of rapacity and force, achieved largely through
the kinetic energy of the verbs, is again achieved through the
poet's scrupulous attention to the wind itself, his sense of its
particular and formidable reality.

This sense of the uniqueness of natural phenomena—objects,
landscapes, creatures, processes—is seldom absent from Stephens's
best nature lyrics. It is the first casualty when, after *Insurrections*,
he comes with unusual suddenness under the influence of so
many new writers. The poet, Austin Clarke, in a private letter to
the present writer, gives the genesis of Stephens's long poem,
'A Prelude and a Song', the second poem in *The Hill of Vision*:
'Thomas MacDonagh once told me that he lent the "Epithala-
mion" of Spenser to Stephens, who was so excited by it that he sat
down and wrote "A Prelude and a Song".' The occasion is
reminiscent of the first night he read Blake and Browning and
immediately wrote twenty-five poems at a sitting. But in the
present case the resulting poem is altogether derivative, because
Stephens is content to take over not only Spenser's pastoral conventions and his symphonic method, but also the imagery, lan-

guage, subject matter and landscape. Alexandrine refrains and Spenserian cadences recur with limp monotony:

> O sunny sky!
> O meadows that the happy clouds are drifting by.
>
> Then come with clamant reeds and improvise,
> With antic dance and savour of the wood
> And all the games ye learned in sunlit solitude.

There is no particularity in the imagery; the landscape, like the weather and the nymphs, is neither English nor Irish but Arcadian. The mood is one of continuous rapture, sustained by conventional invocation of cloud and sun, of 'dancing maids', 'goat-footed satyrs', 'shady ways' and 'breezy summer morns'.

The Spenserian stimulus and the bucolic theme seem to summon the voices of all the major English Romantics. Like Shelley the poet would be 'as a wave impetuous with life', like Keats he sees the clouds 'faintly tinged by the day's afterglow', in a Wordsworthian moment he hears the wind 'By screaming crag or murmurous waterside'. He has suddenly become a sort of Aeolian lyre for the winds of pastoral and Romantic tradition. While the poem has grace and smoothness and is clearly by someone who can write, it can hardly boast a fresh image or original cadence. It is remarkable that a writer of such obvious creative intelligence should, in this phase of his work, show himself so destitute of critical judgment. But we must remember that the year is 1912, and further note that reviewers on both sides of the Irish Sea found no particular fault with either the poem or the tendencies in contemporary poetry which it exemplified. By the time Stephens came to assemble his first *Collected Poems*, in 1926, some of its deficiencies were obvious to him. Only a quarter of 'A Prelude and a Song' is retained, and what remains is dispersed through the book as separate, and not very impressive, independent lyrics. These are 'Follow, Follow, Follow' (p. 11), 'Song, I am Tired to Death' (p. 38), 'If I had Wings Just Like a Bird' (p. 231) and 'No More of Woeful Misery I Sing' (p. 246). With the long last poem in the volume, 'The Lonely God', in which the influences of Milton and AE are incongruously blent, he is as we have seen more ruthless still, suppressing it in its entirety.

His susceptibility to sudden enthusiasm for poets whom he has recently read becomes, if possible, more marked when he accepts Sir Edward Marsh's invitation to be included in his first anthologies of *Georgian Poetry* in 1912, 1915 and 1917. The effect of this association was disastrous for his development in the years immediately ahead. It brought him into the company of English poets who believed that they were in some way revolutionary but who appear in retrospect to have cultivated all the qualities which ran counter to the genuine modern sensibility which Yeats, Pound and Eliot were striving to articulate. Their influence on Stephens was to divert him from those themes—and their attendant technical challenges—which had made his early poetry most strikingly original: his doubts, his defiances, his questioning of social and religious orthodoxies. His early efforts, however unconscious, to develop a poetic language which could cope with the realities of modern experience are now abandoned for a shallow, undemanding lyricism. His poetry, especially in *Songs from the Clay*, becomes one of extrovert celebration, a recital of the delights of nature in which his dangerous facility with sing-song metres and commonplace rhymes is set free from the restraints of genuine thought.

The opening poem from *Songs from the Clay* is all too representative of the book's spirit and content. Entitled 'And it was Windy Weather' it is worth quoting in full for the suggestiveness of its symptoms:

> Now the winds are riding by,
> Clouds are galloping the sky,
> And the trees are lashing their
> Leafy plumes upon the air;
> They are crying as they sway—
> 'Pull the roots out of the clay,
> Dance away, O, dance away;
> Leave the rooted place and speed
> To the hill-side and the mead,
> To the roaring seas we go,
> Chase the airy birds, and know,
> Flying high, flying high,
> All the freedom of the sky,
> All the freedom of the sky.'[2]

The pastoral cliché of 'airy birds', 'leafy plumes', 'hill-sides' and 'meads' are so imprecise that the thinking faculty as well as the visual is virtually suspended. It is 'Georgian' poetry in the worst sense, cheerful, extrovert, escapist, bucolic, elegantly mindless. There is no discernible sense in which the trees can prosper by pulling their roots out of the clay and taking to the sky. Even in Arcady the woods need clay for their sustenance. Even if they managed to obey the poet and transfer from the 'rooted place' to 'the hill-side and the mead' they would have again to put down roots. A poem cannot succeed by grounding itself in meta-phorical nonsense, and this poem, unfortunately, is not untypical of the volume.

The second lyric 'The Rivals' (C.P., p. 10) is equally vacuous. In it the poet and his rival, a bird, compete in singing

> About the dew upon the lawn
> And the wind upon the lea.

In the third, 'The Messenger' (C.P., p. 41, re-titled 'To the Queen of the Bees'), the poet negotiates with a bee in the hope that it will take a message to his beloved. The fourth, entitled 'The Daisies' (C.P., p. 51) is in its way, a fine love lyric despite the conventional nature of its language and imagery:

> In the scented bud of the morning-O
> When the windy grass went rippling far,
> I saw my dear one walking slow,
> In the field where the daisies are.

It represents the better kind of Georgian lyric in the graceful-ness of its rhythm and its delicacy of verbal texture, especially evident in the play of syllables in its second line.

The fifth is a slight love piece about 'an angry maid' who is inevitably 'going down a glade'. The sixth invokes

> The pretty, timid moon and the
> Poor, unhappy little sea.

The objective reality of moon and sea is abolished, they are reduced to mere decorative counters in the poet's self-indulgent reverie.

That Stephens should for a period indulge a mood of escapist pastoralism is understandable in human terms. *Songs from the*

Clay and *The Adventures of Seumas Beg* were written in Paris when he was cut off from his friends and from the literary move-ment that had given him his first self-confidence. They came after a period of intense creative activity: he had produced one large volume of poetry and four substantial works of prose fiction within five years. Suddenly he found himself the first Irish poet elected to what was in effect the most fashionable club in contemporary English letters. It was natural that he should be tempted to understand and imitate their poetic manners. As his letters to Edward Marsh at this period demonstrate, he was regularly and adequately paid for his contributions. That his own work was directly influenced by Hodgson and de la Mare is evident from his letters and from the internal evidence of the poems themselves. But that he should have imitated their vices instead of their modest virtues is a matter of significant regret.[3]

In his booklet on *Poetry in Modern Ireland* Austin Clarke suggests, provokingly, that the success of the Irish 'Celtic Twi-light' may have 'stimulated Walter de la Mare to evoke an English Twilight of his own'.[4] If this be so we can suggest in turn that Stephens re-imported de la Mare's twilight décor to the night pieces in *The Rocky Road to Dublin*.[5] Here, in a series of nostalgic impressions of Dublin streets, parks, river-side and canal-bank scenes, the atmosphere and the lighting are sharply reminiscent of the English poet's transparencies. 'Portobello Bridge' (C.P., p. 103) derives obviously from de la Mare's cele-brated lyric, 'Silver':

> Silver stars shine peacefully!
> The Canal is silver! The
>
> Poplars bear with modest grace
> Gossamers of silver lace!
>
> And the turf bank wears with glee
> Black and silver filigree!

Songs from the Clay contains another such derivation entitled 'Washed in Silver' (C.P., p. 146)

> Gleaming in silver are the hills!
> Blazing in silver is the sea!

And a silvery radiance spills
Where the moon drives royally!

And ends with Stephensian drollery

Clad in silver tissue, I
March magnificently by.

Poems like 'Donnybrook', 'Blue Stars and Gold', 'Merrion Square' and 'Mount Street' repeat with little variation the same pictorial effect.

In October 1913 Ralph Hodgson published his 'Song of Honour' in *The Saturday Review* and dedicated it to Stephens. It began:

I climbed a hill as light fell short,
And rooks came home in scramble sort.[6]

Stephens replied with an extended lyric in the same mood and metre which he published as 'A Reply' in *Songs from the Clay*. Its third movement begins:

You have climbed a hill, and I
Climbed it too; we saw the sun
Toiling up his hill of sky,
Shouting to the night to run
And hide itself before he came
With his scimitar of flame.[7]

It is a fair example of average Georgian verse: the sun's scimitar of flame is initially engaging, but it does not bear close scrutiny; the drama of its stance is undermined when we are forced to see its bearer, an Oriental warrior, 'toiling' upwards. Of course it does not *invite* close scrutiny: it lives for the hearty verbal gesture. We are not therefore surprised by the bland homogeneity of tone with which Hodgson replies yet again in 'I Love a Hill' also dedicated to the Irish poet:

And I can stay at home and find
The hill itself content my mind,
And sup on wonders still . . .
I love a hill for twenty things,
I always take a road that brings
Me halt upon a hill.[8]

To have found a market for verse so routine, unflexed and pedestrian in one of the most prestigious publications of the day proved too strong a temptation for Stephens. And it has been his misfortune that anthologists have chosen to represent him by so many lyrics written under these auspices.

Hodgson, Munro, de la Mare and their school wrote copiously about animals, their charm, their beauty, their sufferings at man's hands. Hodgson's famous and humane lyric, 'The Bells of Heaven', remains one of the most anthologised of modern poems with its plea

> For tamed and shabby tigers
> And dancing dogs and bears,
> And wretched, blind pit ponies,
> And little hunted hares.

This theme enters Stephens's work for the first time in *Songs from the Clay* with a piece which has achieved almost equal celebrity, 'The Snare':

> And I cannot find the place
> Where his paw is in the snare!
> Little one! Oh, little one!
> I am searching everywhere.

His attitude to 'little things' had been far from sentimental in *The Demi-Gods* where MacCann's treatment of the ass and the spider's reflections on the blue-bottle had been closer to the untroubled primitivism of Synge than to the Society for the Prevention of Cruelty to Animals. In a short poem entitled 'Little Things'—a curious adaptation of the Lord's Prayer—written some years later, Stephens comes back to the theme:

> All trapped and frightened little things,
> The mouse, the coney, hear our prayer!
>
> As we forgive those done to us,
> —The lamb, the linnet, and the hare—
>
> Forgive us all our trespasses,
> Little creatures, everywhere![9]

Writing specifically about the Georgian school of poetry, T. S.

Eliot remarks in 1917 that 'it is not unworthy to notice how often the word "little" occurs; and how this word is used, not merely as a piece of information, but with a caress, a conscious delight'.[10] The word has turned up repeatedly in the excerpts quoted—they were not chosen with this point in mind—and always in the manner Eliot suggests. Whether it is predicated of 'the poor un- happy little sea' or of hares and coneys it always carries a sense of overt tenderness if not outright sentimentality. Along with this goes an unconscious condescension to the world outside the poet's mind. Life and its occurrences, nature and its processes, are tamed and reduced by the caress of poetic cliché.

It would be possible, but ultimately unfruitful, to trace in detail the interactions of the Georgian poets upon one another and the shameless borrowings and exchanges that took place between them especially while the *Georgian Poetry* anthologies continued. The role of Stephens in such a catalogue would be considerable. It is, however, enough to record that between the years of 1912 and 1916, when he returned to Dublin, Stephens conducted what can best be described as a dalliance with the English school of Georgian poets. We shall see how he escaped from the worst aspects of their influence, and also how he never quite shook off their tendency towards ornate and mannered cliché when confronted with the natural world in both its humbler and its grander manifestations.

There were of course areas of Georgian influence from which he was necessarily excluded : he had no access to their enthusiasm for county cricket, country houses or rectories in Grandchester. The fact that the English country lane and the Sussex downs were 'terra incognita' to the expatriate Irishman may account for the fact that a purely literary landscape of leas, meads and lawns dominates the scenery of his nature poetry. He could not share their patriotic fervour for England's cause in the Great War, though we shall see how the influence of Rupert Brooke asserted itself in his elegy for the dead of Easter Week written after his return to Ireland in 1915.

What their influence cut him off from is more significant. It was unfortunate that he never seemed to respond to the anti- war poetry of Wilfred Owen and Siegfried Sassoon, even after Sassoon's poetry had appeared side by side with his own in the Georgian anthology of 1917. It was unfortunate that he chose deliberately to reject Eliot and Pound, and that their lessons for the modern poetic sensibility never found a way into his poetic practice. In the face of these refusals the way forward for Stephens had to be the way back : the discovery of a body of Gaelic poetry which he felt impelled to translate and which in turn sent him back to the hard colloquial idiom of *Insurrections* for a language in which to render it.

But the overall impact of *Songs from the Clay* and *The Rocky Road to Dublin* can be summed up in Eliot's dismissive catalogue of the stock Georgian images. Essentially a poetry of 'rainbows, cuckoos, daffodils and timid hares', it is narrow in its scope, vague and often archaic in its language, pedestrian in its rhythms, shallow in its sentiment, derivative in its imagery. Fortunately it constitutes only an interlude in the poet's development. And happily the second of the two volumes is enlivened by the childhood visions of Seumas Beg in which Stephens's true voice is consistently audible.

The Child's Perspective

Seumas Beg, as persona, appears in a poem of that name in Stephens's first volume, *Insurrections*; he had, therefore, a foothold on the poet's imagination before the surge of influence that followed on its publication. Most of the Seumas Beg poems were published before 1912, three years before Stephens got them together in one book. It is therefore not surprising that these evocations of childhood are closer to the childhood lyrics of Wordsworth and Blake than to the children's poetry of de la Mare. In a letter to Marsh in 1915 Stephens is insistent that 'they are not verses for children'.[11] Significantly in his *Collected Poems* he places the majority of them at the end of his fourth book, 'Heels and Head' where he assembles most of his visionary lyrics.

Both Blake and Wordsworth had seen the child as especially blessed—innocent, wise and imaginative, close to the eternal sources of truth, beauty and love. Before the onslaught of 'experience', the 'shades of the prison house', the child presented an image of unfallen man, of the undefiled imagination, uncorrupted by sin and uncomplicated by reason whether it be defined in terms of Blake's 'vegetable ratio' or Wordsworth's 'meddling intellect'.

Stephens's idea of the childhood state, whether it be derived or original, incorporates these Romantic attributions. His notion of human wisdom is that of resolutely fighting against the corruptions of adulthood, against the artificialities of 'civilisation', its rationalities, ethics and prohibitions which constitute for him the essence of man's modern 'prison house'. The genuinely wise among his fictive personalities fall into four categories, all of which evade or defeat the imperatives of organised morality : there are those who are mad, and therefore invincibly ignorant of ethical prescription, like Mad Patsy who refuses to work because he wants to play with angels in the Poppy Field in a poem of that name. Patsy rejects the voice of ethical man :

> —A poppy is a devil weed,—
> I said to him—he disagreed . . .
> The devil has not any flower,
> But only money in his power.

There are society's outlaws whether predatory, like Patsy Mac-Cann—a man almost corrupted by the prospect of money—mendicant, like Billy the Music, or merely subversive, like Mac-Dhoul. There are those who yield themselves with ideal Blakean spontaneity to natural desire like Caitilin in *The Crock of Gold* and Eileen in *The Demi-Gods*. Finally there are the children who are by nature spared from the attritions of social responsibility; as can be seen in *The Crock of Gold* and in 'Three Happy Places'—from *Here Are Ladies*—children have the added gift of wonder and therefore of unlimited imaginative energy.

The centrality of the childhood vision to Stephens's work is first expressed in a deceptively simple lyric from *The Hill of Vision* entitled 'I Wish' (C.P., p. 166) aptly placed before the 'Seumas Beg' poems in the collected edition :

> I wish I had not come to man's estate,
> I wish I was a silly urchin still,
> With bounding pulses, and a heart elate
> To meet whatever came of good or ill.
>
> Of good or ill ! Not knowing what was good,
> But groping to a better than I knew;
> And guessing deeper than I understood;
> And hoping truths that seemed to be untrue.

> Of good or ill! When it so often seems,
> There is no good at all but only ill.
> Alas, the sunny summer-time of dreams!
> The dragons I had nerved my hand to kill!
> The maid I could have rescued, and the queen
> Whose champion long ago I might have been.

Here experience has brought with it two related misfortunes: the ethical perplexity of 'good and ill', and a diminution of the child's intuitive capacities to guess, imagine and create. That these two are related almost to the point of identity has been dramatised in his progressive exploration of the ethical problem in the poetry and the prose fantasy. What the Seumas Beg lyrics enact is the poet's attempt to recover, by the imaginative act of re-creation, the mood in which the child could make the external world bow to its sense of wonder and receive the impress of its heightened perceptions and imaginations. They are his songs of innocence and of experience and the impulse behind them is no less imperative because they are executed humorously and often with irony:

> A man was sitting underneath a tree
> Outside the village; and he asked me what
> Name was upon this place; and said that he
> Was never here before—He told a lot
>
> Of stories to me too. His nose was flat!
> I asked him how it happened, and he said
> —The first mate of the Holy Ghost did that
> With a marling-spike one day; but he was dead,
>
> And jolly good job too; and he'd have gone
> A long way to have killed him— Oh, he had
> A gold ring in one ear; the other one
> —'Was bit off by a crocodile, bedad!'
>
> That's what he said. He taught me how to chew!
> He was a real nice man! He liked me too![12]

The technical achievement here need hardly be stressed: the voices of the fascinated urchin and the chatty traveller work in easy and authentic counterpoint. The child's sense of the exotic and the fabulous as it plays over the flat nose, the earring, the strange name of the ship, the adventures of the sailor with the first mate and the crocodile, is comically real. And the incident is neatly and unexpectedly shaped to the form of a Shakespearian sonnet.

The Seumas Beg epiphanies—weirdly reminiscent of Joyce's first three stories in *Dubliners*[13]—all hinge on the child's ability to observe, transfigure and create. Their poles of significance are what Robert Farren has called the 'blasting realism'[14] of children on the one hand and on the other their ability to irradiate the commonplace with their aura of romance. It is part of Stephens's secret as a writer of fantasy in prose and verse that he retained these capacities to an exceptional degree.

In 'The Turn of the Road'[15] the child suddenly comes upon an old woman, a Bessie Bobtail figure, searching among the bushes:

> She was wrinkle-faced. She had big teeth.—The end
> Of her shawl caught on a bush and rolled
> Right off her, and her hair fell down—Her face
> Was white, and awful, and her eyes looked sick,
> And she was talking queer.
> '*O God of Grace*!'
> Said she, '*Where is the child*?' And flew back quick
> The way she came, and screamed, and shook her hands!
> ... Maybe she was a witch from foreign lands.

The facts are first dramatically registered, and in the last line the process of fantasy, of myth-making, is already under way in the observer's imagination. But before the saving grace of fancy enters, the child's sense of the distraught woman has been rendered in blunt colloquial language. This return to simple direct speech makes these poems superior to the facile poeticism of the nature lyrics, and each of the childhood visions more riveting than the last.

The terrifying adult in 'The Apple Tree' is imbued with the same tangible and energetic reality:

> He panted like a horse! His eyes were queer!
> Wide-open! Staring frightfully! And, hist!
> His mouth stared open like another eye!
> And all his hair was matted down with sweat!

In 'The Devil's Bag' (C.P., p. 168) a recollection of childhood
dread, inspired by a now discarded theology, comes back with
the same concrete force: this is not the wan, apologetic Satan
of the visionary lyrics but the ghoulish creature used to frighten
children:

> I saw the Devil walking down the lane
> Behind our house—A heavy bag
> Was strapped upon his shoulders and the rain
> Sizzled when it hit him . . .
> He picked a rag,
> Up from the ground and put it in his sack,
> And grinned, and rubbed his hands.
> There was a thing
> Alive inside the bag upon his back
> —It must have been a soul! I saw it fling
> And twist about inside, and not a hole
> Or cranny for escape! Oh, it was sad.
> I cried, and shouted out,—*Let out that soul!*—
> But he turned round, and, sure, his face went mad,
> And twisted up and down, and he said 'Hell!'
> And ran away . . . Oh, mammy! I'm not well.

The last line is more than a comic anti-climax: it comes as a
necessary release from the oppressive fear created in the body of
the poem, by the twist and fling of the verbs, the dramatic sense
of immediacy, the grotesque particularity of the images in which
the devil and his captive are evoked. The giant who tries to
capture the child in 'In the Orchard' (C.P., p. 174) is registered
in the same strenuous, concrete idiom:

> He held a blackthorn club in his right hand,
> And plunged the other into every tree,
> Searching for something—You could stand
> Beside him and not reach up to his knee,
> So big he was—I trembled lest he should
> Come trampling, round-eyed, down to where I stood.

The experience lives in the action, the vigour of movement, in
the swift succession of 'held', 'plunged', 'Searching', 'stand',
'reach', and in the dramatic counterpoise of 'trembling' with

'trampling'. Throughout these lyrics one is aware of the story-teller's talent, the flair for character, narrative and vivid local detail. Above all for the conclusion withheld, the sudden reversal at the end. This quality which we have seen most notably in the macabre climax of 'Nora Crionna' achieves a similar effect at the end of 'Behind the Hill' where a fabulous and apparently benign 'man in green' beguiles Seumas Beg—having established that his mother is absent—with chat about a castle and a crock of gold which the child may have if he comes with him:

> ...so, off we went.
> He said he had a pound hid in the crock,
> And owned the castle too, and paid no rent
> To anyone, and that you had to knock
> Five hundred times. I asked, *'Who reckoned up?'*
> And he said, *'You insulting little pup!'*

Even with the difference in *genre* the poem is uncannily reminiscent of 'An Encounter' in which the child's inner desire for the romance of the Norwegian sailors with green eyes ends with his looking into the murky green eyes of a sinister old man who also suffers an unexpected change of mood, thereby revealing a side of his nature far from romantic.

The epiphanies of Seumas Beg are emphatically, as the author insists, not 'verses for children'. They enforce a continuous dialogue between the child's yearning for the wonder tale, for the imagined land of romance and triumphant adventure—'The dragons I had nerved my hand to kill'—and on the other hand the world of everyday reality, benign, squalid or malignant, in which they must live. They enact a sense of childhood innocence and, with equal force, the child's vulnerability. They are the products of a poetic imagination that is equally conversant with the dream of idyllic happiness and the nightmare of guilt and terror. That is to say that their peculiar merit as poems, their tense direct idiom, their economy, their authenticity of character, incident and place, their concentration and finish as verbal constructs, derive from a felt experience of childhood that remains urgent and active in the mind of the mature writer going about his imaginative task.

7

Stephens and the Easter Rising

The Poet as Reporter

In September 1915 Stephens returned with his family to
Dublin to take up his post as Registrar of the National Gallery.
The move marks a curious watershed in his writing career. In
the months before his return, his letters from Paris, especially
those to Thomas Bodkin whose influence secured him the appointment, indicate a strange tangle of doubts, resolutions and hesitations as to his future course as a writer. In March 1915 he wrote
to his friend that he proposed a 'Comedie Humaine of Ireland':

> What a story there is to tell there. None of our men seem
> aware of the passionate, varied story that Ireland is & has
> been, but 'is' for me who am modern & interested almost
> entirely in things I can touch and feel. My plan is to take a
> slice of Irish time, say the twenty years culminating in this day
> & the tomorrows during which I will be writing & explore
> these, with the particularity of a grub working through an
> apple, until I have attained to a consciousness of Ireland in all
> its dimensions, & which consciousness I can impress, not alone
> into my books, but into our people—Behold a Job!¹

Before the month was out he declared, again in a letter to
Bodkin, 'I really think my poetry days are over', and quoted a
remark of AE that you cannot eat your poetic cake in prose and
have it afterwards in verse. 'As to the Balzac scheme,' he continued, 'I am quite ready to disavow that too-heroic advertise-
ment, but I'll try it first.' By June he had no new book in process :
'I can't write here & have almost forgotten that I ever could
write.'

From these and from other comments of this time it is

obvious that Stephens had completed a decisive stage in his literary output, and that he was groping for some new mode of apprehension which might revitalise his artistic impulse. In the event it took the form neither of extended realistic fiction nor of a flight from poetry, though it emphatically did involve 'a new consciousness of Ireland'.

Nine months after his return to Dublin, in April 1916, the Easter Rising took place almost literally outside his window. Within a matter of months he had published his prose diary of Easter Week and a small volume of poems also occasioned by the Rebellion and entitled *Green Branches*. During the ten years that followed he devoted his energies to the imaginative recovery of Ireland's poetic and mythological past. There can be little doubt that the impact of the military and political upheaval provided him with a fresh inspiration and pointed the new direction that he had been hoping for in his final letters from Paris.

The Insurrection in Dublin[2] remains a fascinating book for several reasons. The day-to-day reporting, wherein the author moves restlessly around the streets, recording accurately the incidents he witnesses and describing the rumours and speculations of his fellow citizens, takes up two-thirds of the volume. These impressions, observed and recorded with his sharp writer's eye in spare and precise prose are as fresh and vivid as when first written. They convey the terror, the absurdity and the bewilderment of a civilian population caught in the trauma of sudden and unexpected revolution. Unique in the documents of the period they look forward to O'Casey's vision of the city in the last two acts of *The Plough and the Stars*. Their dramatic quality derives chiefly from the presence of the writer himself, a quiet, questioning observer treading his way vigilantly through the chaos and the danger. A dreadful incident in which the Volunteers first draw blood before his eyes is starkly described. A stubborn and uncomprehending civilian goes forward to the barricade at Stephen's Green corner to retrieve a hand-lorry which has been commandeered by the insurgents:

> The man walked directly towards the Volunteers, who, to the number of about ten, were lining the railings. He walked slowly, bent a little forward, with one hand raised and one finger up as though he were going to make a speech. Ten guns

were pointing at him and a voice repeated many times: 'Go
and put back that lorry or you are a dead man. Go before I
count four. One, two, three, four . . .' A rifle spat at him, and
in two undulating movements the man sank on himself and
sagged to the ground. I ran to him with some others, while a
woman screamed unmeaningly, all on one strident note. The
man was picked up and carried to a hospital beside the Arts
Club. There was a hole in the top of his head, and one does
not know how ugly blood can look until it has been seen
clotted in hair. As the poor man was being carried in, a
woman plumped to her knees in the road and began not to
scream but to screech. At that moment the Volunteers were
hated.

In its spareness of description and its graphic sense of significant
detail it foreshadows the kind of reporting that writers like John
Hersey were to develop in the later journalism of the century.
The detail, as the diary proceeds, is by turns homely, tragic,
grotesque and plaintive: a boy clutching a ham which for days
he has been trying to get to his sister in Sackville Street; a dead
horse lying 'stiff and lamentable' for days on the footpath; a
pretty working-class girl haranguing the onlookers in 'the most
obscene language which I have ever heard'; the willingness of
everyone to exchange news, the equal determination not to offer
a political opinion; the comic portrait of a figure out of
O'Casey who 'spat rumour as though his mouth were a machine
gun . . . the only thoroughly happy person in our city':

He said the Germans had landed in three places. One of these
landings alone consisted of fifteen thousand men. The other
landings probably beat that figure. The whole city of Cork was
in the hands of the Volunteers, and, to that extent, might be
said to be peaceful. German warships had defeated the English,
and their transports were speeding from every side. The whole
country was up, and the garrison was outnumbered by one
hundred to one.

Though his description of the fighting, the street scenes, the
reactions of the citizens, the atmosphere of rumour and counter
rumour is largely objective and dispassionate, Stephens's imaginative sympathy with the insurrection reveals itself in occasional

flashes. An early member of Griffith's *Sinn Féin* and a student of Irish, he cannot help seeing the insurrection as another chapter in his country's struggle for independence. One passage in particular conveys this sense of sympathy and dramatises the gradual swing of spectator opinion towards the embattled Volunteers: 'People say: "Of course, they will be beaten". The statement is almost a query, and they continue, "but they are putting up a decent fight". For being beaten does not greatly matter in Ireland, but not fighting does matter. "They went forth always to battle; and they always fell." Indeed the history of the Irish race is in that phrase.' This is history as seen through the prism of national myth as it had been expressed in Yeats's *Cathleen ni Houlihan* and in the Easter Proclamation itself.

This Republican bias becomes overt in the second, more polemical, section of the book in Stephens's bitter attack on the leader of the Irish Parliamentary Party at Westminster, John Redmond, for pledging Ireland's support for Britain at the outbreak of the Great War:

> On the day of the declaration of war between England and Germany he took the Irish case, weighty with eight centuries of history and tradition, and threw it out of the window. . . . He swore Ireland to loyalty as if he had Ireland in his pocket, and could answer for her. . . . Mr Redmond told the lie and he is answerable to England for the violence she had been guilty of, and to Ireland for the desolation to which we have had to submit. Without his lie there had been no Insurrection; without it there had been at this moment, and for a year past, an end to the 'Irish Question'. Ireland must in ages gone have been guilty of abominable crimes or she could not at this juncture have been afflicted with a John Redmond.

Historians must judge the truth of this severe indictment. Stephens's argument is that if Redmond had declared for Ireland 'a benevolent neutrality' England would have within months offered Home Rule in return for Irish soldiers. The political situation, however, in Ireland south and north, and in Britain, was more complex than Stephens's account acknowledges. And his ascripiton of such large culpability to John Redmond for the insurrection is clearly excessive.

Stephens's pen-portraits of the leaders are brief, accurate and vivid. He had known MacDonagh and Plunkett intimately as collaborators on *The Irish Review*, the O'Rahilly, Connolly and Pearse, less well as acquaintances. His comments on the mysterious personality of Pearse are as close to Pearse's character as the historian is likely to get:

> I think that Pearse became the leader because his temperament was more profoundly emotional than any of the others. He was emotional not in a flighty, but in a serious way, and one felt more that he suffered than that he enjoyed.
>
> He had a power; men who came into intimate contact with him began to act differently to their own desires and interests.

He ends his discussion of the leaders with the assertion that they were temperamentally reluctant to undertake such 'bloody and desolate work' : 'one can imagine them say "Oh! cursed spite", as they accepted the responsibility.' The one man of whom this was not plainly true, however, was Pearse whose overt messianic doctrine of blood sacrifice had played such a crucial part in bringing the rebellion to a head.

What strikes one most about the book is the confident seriousness of the author's tone. Stephens's status as a foremost Irish writer is everywhere in evidence. Like Shaw and Yeats he speaks with the assumed authority of a man of letters whose word carries weight and must be listened to. Thus his final appeal is to the English statesmen and to the people of Ireland. To the former he makes a plea for swift conciliatory action : 'A peace that will last forever can be made with Ireland if you wish to make it, but you must take her hand at once, for in a few months' time she will not open it to you; the old, bad relations will re-commence, the rancour will be born and grow, and another memory will be stored away in Ireland's capacious and retentive brain.' The years that followed were to bear out this prophecy all too precisely. The paragraph on which the book ends is addressed to his fellow-countrymen and is a plea for a fresh application of the *Sinn Féin* doctrine :

> Irishmen must begin to think for themselves and of themselves, instead of expending energy on causes too distant to be assisted or hindered by them ... We have more problems to resolve in our towns and cities than many generations of minds will get

tired of striving with. Here is the world, and all that perplexes or delights the world is here also. Nothing is lost. Not even brave men. They have been used. From this day the great adventure opens for Ireland. The Volunteers are dead, and the call is now for volunteers.

Taken all in all *The Insurrection in Dublin* is a trenchant, perceptive and courageous book. When we recall that Stephens held a prominent public office the full degree of his courage in speaking out in a cause that seemed irreparably lost becomes the more apparent. His energies as a writer have been vigorously revived and that 'Irish consciousness' of which he wrote in his Paris letters is now awake and combative.

Elegy and Re-Birth

Green Branches is a suite of public poems occasioned by the Easter Rising and the subsequent execution of the leaders. It is elaborately ceremonial, shaped in terms of seasonal imagery wherein the despair of its first component, 'Autumn 1915' is followed by the resurgence of hope in 'Spring 1916', and rounded off in the final sonnet, 'Joy be with us' which employs the metaphor of a voyage and a plea to the Irish sea god Mannanaan. The form is that of the pastoral elegy moving from death, through resurrection to a final hopeful apotheosis. The language is, inevitably perhaps, conventional, redolent of the Georgian cadences that had dominated Stephens's poetry in his two most recent volumes. Its attempt at an orchestral unity fails and the failure is acknowledged in the *Collected Poems* where the first movement is separated from the others and presented as an independent and not very impressive lyric.

Yet the volume is strangely interesting for one following the curve of Stephens's development as a poet. One senses in it an end and a beginning. 'Autumn 1915' on one level may be seen as an elaborate exercise in scene-setting, an extended pathetic fallacy in which nature bodies forth in its sense of seasonal decay the despair of Ireland :

> The Spring will never come again,
> And there is end of everything—
>
> Day after day
> The sap will ebb away . . .

On another level it is a personal poem in which the poet seems to be saying goodbye to the nature poetry of the previous years. He dramatises himself, in the Romantic convention of Wordsworth's Immortality ode or Coleridge's ode on Dejection, as a solitary, seeking in nature the inspiration which has faded from the earth:

> For I had clung,
> —With what of laughter and of eagerness!—
> Unto the hope that I might chance to be
> Master of Song! And, singing, be no less
> Than those great poets of antiquity,
> Who sang the clouds and hills; of stars and clods;
> Of trees and streams, and the mind and soul of man;
> And chaunted too the universal gods . . .

The poem proceeds through the gestures of conventional melancholy and disenchantment: the poet, now 'a saddened elf', drops from his hands 'this tuneful reed' and takes his last look at 'that most lovely land'. If it were not followed by the formal patriotic elegy of 'Spring 1916' the poem might be taken as an extended, and rather wan, valedictory on nature lyricism. And it is as such that it appears in the *Collected Poems*.

'Spring 1916', while suffering from the defects of the same Georgian diction, has considerably more force, and carries, in its better passages, genuine conviction and passion. After its ceremonial opening with the conventional 'flower passage', it invokes Spring in a complex image of flags and branches:

> At springing of the year you came and swung
> Green flags above the newly-greening earth;
> Scarce were the leaves unfolded, they were young,
> Nor had outgrown the wrinkles of their birth:
> Comrades they thought you of their pleasant hour,
> Who had but glimpsed the sun when they saw you!
> Who heard your song ere birds had singing power,
> And drank your blood or e'er they drank the dew.

The symbolism of blood sacrifice so prominent in the contemporary writings of nationalist poets, English and Irish, but especially Pearse's reiterated conviction that the 'old heart of the earth needed to be warmed with the red wine of the battle-fields', is clearly present in Stephens's rhetoric. In Yeats's 'The Rose Tree' one finds further evidence of how quickly this sanguinary concept was absorbed into the poetic consciousness once the smoke of insurrection had cleared.

The elegy goes on to develop the notion of the young nation and the return of spring: older nations salute their dead with 'drums and trumpets' and 'with pacing cortege': Ireland will, more appropriately, honour the dead patriots with the symbolic fruits of spring:

> We have no drums or trumpets! Naught have we,
> But some green branches taken from a tree,
> And flowers that grow at large in mead and vale!

The last movement, 'Joy be with us', in loose sonnet form, changes the imagery to that of a ship making from harbour:

> Be ye propitious, winds of destiny!
> On us at first blow not too boisterous bold
> All Ireland hath is packed into this hold.
>
> Her hopes fly at the peak! Now it is dawn
> And we away—be with us Mananán!

It is difficult to judge *Green Branches* as poetry. The elegiac form is archaic and derivative, its pastoral conventions at odds with the actuality of the occasion in the manner of Yeats's 'Shepherd and Goatherd'. Its deployment of the contemporary patriotic images of blood sacrifice, the dawn, spring and the Celtic sea-god is deliberately mythopoeic, its language consciously 'poetic' and ceremonial. It evinces, however, a new sense of energy and purpose in the poet's attitude to experience. It can best be seen as a poem of transition between the nature poetry of his Georgian phase and the work in translation, reincarnation and mythic recension that is to come.

8

Reincarnations

The Rhetoric of Complaint
The title of Stephens's 1918 volume of poetry, *Reincarnations*, gives the most valuable clue to his methods as a translator: he is primarily interested in the personalities behind the poems he chooses to translate and adapt. In his renderings the characters of O'Bruadair and O'Rahilly in particular reveal themselves with remarkable individuality. Those of their poems he selects for translation reveal one aspect of their character and predicament which has been active in Stephens's writing so far. This is the theme of social complaint, more especially the poet's complaint against a materialistic society which shows no respect for his ministry. These lines from O'Rahilly's 'The Land of Fal' might easily be mistaken for a passage in *Insurrections*:

> Why are the poor tormented? Why made grieve
> The innocent? Why the free enslaved?
> Why have the wicked peace though void of truth?[1]

The poverty of O'Bruadair in the seventeenth century had its historical causes: the Gaelic chieftains quitted Ireland after the Battle of Kinsale in 1601 and he was left without a patron. O'Rahilly inherited an even more impoverished world after the broken Treaty of Limerick in 1691. Both were of old bardic families and their poetry combines anger with a nostalgia for a world in which poets had been greatly respected. In Stephens's renderings, while the historical context is not ignored, it is kept in a minor key. The result is that these Gaelic poets are in a sense reincarnated as types of the alienated artist in every human context.

The challenge therefore was to find a language and a style which would not betray the historical situation of the originals and at the same time reconstitute them as modern poems. This challenge was less testing when the occasion of the original was simple and immediate, as in O'Bruadair's argument with a weaver or a barmaid about his inability to pay the bill in poems like 'The Weavers' and 'A Glass of Beer'; it was more demanding when the original mourned the passing of the Gaelic chieftains and a golden age that had gone forever, as in O'Bruadair's bitter complaint translated under the title 'Skim Milk' or O'Rahilly's lament for the MacCarthys translated as 'The Wave of Cliona'. In the latter kind of poem something of the archaic, elegiac idiom of the original had to be insinuated into the modern and colloquial language necessary to make the poem immediate and contemporary. Stephens's success in both areas is outstanding: the simpler emotions find expression in direct conversational language stripped of ornament and archaism; the latter in a careful counterpoint of that idiom against a 'high style', a blend that is most triumphantly achieved in 'Skim Milk'—arguably the finest of Stephens's poems—and a dramatic lyric entitled 'Egan O'Rahilly'.

David O'Bruadair

In his *Collected Poems* Stephens refuses to accord the lyrics of *Reincarnations* any special status as translations; and though most of them are gathered in Book V, 'Less than Daintily', for thematic reasons, he clearly wishes the reader to encounter them as independent poems. It is therefore useful to name the poems which are derived from the originals of the Gaelic poets in question: O'Bruadair's are 'An Apology', 'The Weavers', 'A Glass of Beer', 'Blue Blood', 'Odell', 'The Geraldine's Cloak', 'Skim Milk', 'O'Bruadair', and 'The Gang' which is not included in the collected edition.

In a letter to an American friend in 1917 he wrote:

There is a man named O'Bruadair who lived and sang and was very hungry and exceedingly thirsty in the time of Cromwell, Crumwell as we call him and with whose name we inevitably link the worst of our curses. But O'Bruadair is gorgeous, a very learned man and a very poor one, a man who was devout and thirsty in equal and terrific extreme. I have never met such an avalanche of eloquence, poetry and rage under the one skin.[2]

'An Apology', the first poem in the O'Bruadair suite, establishes at once the poet's character and his precarious position in the social order of his times. He has got drunk at the house of one of his rare patrons and composes a ceremonial apology to his host, arguing that 'it is the poet's failing to incline, / By nature and by art to jolity.' Because the occasion is formal the language and tone are eloquent, bardic and nostalgic:

> Always I loved to see—sight all too rare—!
> The rich red tide lip at a flagon's brim;
> To sit, half fool and half philosopher;
> To chat with every kind of her and him;
> And shrug at lore of money-gatherer.
>
> Often I trudge the mud by hedge and wall!
> And often there's no money in my purse!
> Nor malice in my heart ever at all!
> And of my songs no person is the worse,
> But I myself, who give my all to all.

When the occasion is less ceremonial, as in 'A Glass of Beer', Stephens brings into play a sort of 'low style' equally appropriate to his theme. Here the poet has been forcibly expelled from a public house for having requested a drink on credit from the barmaid:

> The lanky hank of a she in the inn over there
> Nearly killed me for asking the loan of a glass of beer;
> May the devil grip the whey-faced slut by the hair,
> And beat bad manners out of her skin for a year.

Here the tough, colloquial language which had given such force to his early dramatic lyrics comes back with increased energy and concentration. In the note to *Reincarantions* Stephens's remarks that O'Bruadair 'lets out of him an unending rebellious bawl which would be the most desolating utterance ever made by man if it was not also the most gleeful.' This quality of glee is especially released in the dramatic situations, the physical and verbal confrontations between the impoverished Gaelic poet and his enemies within the social order:

That parboiled ape, with the toughest jaw you would see
On virtue's path, and a voice that would rasp the dead,
Came roaring and raging the minute she looked at me,
And threw me out of the house on the back of my head!

The same sense of urgent vocal argument between the poet and
his society asserts itself in 'The Weavers':

You weave good shirts, and I weave, for my bread,
Good poetry—But you get paid at times.
The only rap I get is on my head:
And when it comes again that men like rhymes
—And pay for them—I'll pay you for your shirt!

The contemptuous refusal to provide a rhyme on the last beat
can perhaps be taken as the poet's impatient dismissal of his
opponent as he departs.

The incessant theme of the O'Bruadair poems is the theme
that Yeats takes up twenty years later, in an idiom strongly
reminiscent of Stephens, in his great ballad 'The Curse of
Cromwell' which is regarded by many as his closest approxima-
tion to the quality of the traditional Irish poets, the best
example of that 'Irish style' which he so often referred to in his
critical writings:

You ask what I have found, and far and wide I go;
Nothing but Cromwell's house and Cromwell's
                                    murderous crew,
The lovers and the dancers are beaten into the clay,
And the tall men and the swordsmen and the horsemen,
                                    where are they?
And there is an old beggar wandering in his pride.
His fathers served their fathers before Christ was
                                    crucified.

O'Bruadair's debate is also with 'Cromwell's murderous crew'
and the philistine world that they have created. In 'Blue Blood' a
representative of Cromwell's new aristocracy is lampooned as

—That silly, sulky, illiterate, black-avised boor
Who was hatched by foreign vulgarity under the hedge.

'Odell' which attacks another functionary of the new dispensation closes on a note of combined bitterness and nostalgia:

E

> I pray to Him who, in the haughty hour
> Of Babel, threw confusion on each tongue,
> That I may see our princes back in power,
> And see Odell, the tax-collector, hung!

Both poems, together with 'A Glass of Beer' are included in Yeats's selection from Stephens for *The Oxford Book of Modern Verse* in 1936, the year before 'The Curse of Cromwell' was first published.

The two finest poems in the O'Bruadair sequence are 'O'Bruadair' and 'Skim Milk'. Both concern the poet's predicament, historical and existential, and both draw their strength from a skilful counterpoint of Stephens's two voices, the bardic and the colloquial. 'O'Bruadair' is the Gaelic poet's bitter valedictory on the craft of verse:

> I will sing no more songs! The pride of my country I sang
> Through forty long years of good rhyme, without any
> avail;
> And no one cared even the half of the half of a hang
> For the song or the singer—so, here is an end to the tale.
>
> If you say, if you think, I complain, and have not got a
> cause,
> Let you come to me here, let you look at the state of
> my hand!
> Let you say if a goose-quill has calloused these horny old
> paws,
> Or the spade that I grip on and dig with, out there in the
> land?

In the fourth stanza a sharp contrast is achieved between the speaker's degradation and the world of fine rhetoric which he has been deprived of:

> I ask of the Craftsman that fashioned the fly and the
> bird;
> Of the Champion whose passion will lift me from death
> in time;
> Of the Spirit that melts icy hearts with the wind of a
> word,

That my people be worthy, and get, better singing than
mine.

The last stanza subsides on a note of blended bitterness and
despair in which the two voices meet in a common idiom:

I had hoped to live decent, when Ireland was quit of her
care,
As a poet or steward, perhaps, in a house of degree,
But my end of the tale is—old brogues and old breeches
to wear!
So I'll sing no more songs for the men who care nothing
for me.

These O'Bruadair poems do not lend themselves to the modern
process of 'verbal analysis'; they are so simple, direct and surefooted in their expression, so certain in their purpose and method,
that the consummate skill of their execution is, perhaps too
easily, taken for granted. They are perhaps most striking in their
range of tone, moving through bitterness, astringency, rage, mockery, humour, irony, nostalgia and dignified complaint, and their
skilful avoidance of sentimentality and self-pity. Perhaps the
greatest range of feeling and tone is exhibited in 'Skim Milk', a
poem which has been undeservedly neglected: I quote it in full:

A small part only of my grief I write;
And if I do not publish all the tale
It is because my gloom gets some respite
By just a small bewailing: I bewail
That a poet must with stupid folk abide
Who steal his food and ruin his inside.

Once I had books, each book beyond compare,
And now no book at all is left to me;
Now I am spied and peeped on everywhere
And this old head, stuffed with latinity,
Rich with the poet's store of grave and gay,
Will not get me skim milk for half a day.

A horse, a mule, an ass—no beast have I!
Into the forest day by day I go,
And trot beneath a load of wood, that high!
Which raises on my poor old back a row

Of red raw blisters till I cry—Alack,
The rider that rides me will break my back!

When he was old, and worn, and near his end
The poet met Saint Patrick, and was stayed!
I am a poet too, and seek a friend;
A prop, a staff, a comforter, an aid;
A Patrick to lift Ossian from despair,
In Cormac Uasail mac Donagh of the Golden Hair.

The poem's success derives in great measure from the subtle
counterpoint of two kinds of language. The words 'grief',
'bewail', 'gloom' and 'respite' are the language of formal bardic
complaint, suitable to a poet addressing his patron, conscious of
the dignity of his calling. The two lines with which the first
stanza ends abruptly shift the tone to one of immediate, out-
spoken annoyance. The second stanza works to a similar pattern in
its juxtaposition of latinity and fine books with a world of skim
milk and petty informers. The third stanza, in preparation for
the formal appeal of the last, employs the low style throughout
to register the rude detail of the speaker's physical hardship.
In the last the language rises to the grand manner: the poet
speaks in the idiom of his vocation, calling to witness the tradition
to which he and his patron properly belong. The last line with
its euphonious roll of proper nouns makes a suitably ceremonious
close.

Egan O'Rahilly

The poems that derive from the Irish of O'Rahilly, and which
survive into the *Collected Poems*, are 'Eileen, Diarmuid and
Teig', 'The Wave of Cliona', 'Inis Fal', and 'Egan O'Rahilly'.
The first is a personal elegy for three children, the remaining
three combine personal complaint with lament for the Gaelic
order which is now little more than a distant memory in the
racial consciousness. 'Egan O'Rahilly' is the poem which most
clearly defines the Gaelic poet's stance and outlook; together
with 'Inis Fal' it is included in Yeats's Oxford Book selections:

Here in a distant place I hold my tongue;
I am O'Rahilly!

When I was young,
Who now am young no more,

I did not eat things picked up from the shore :
The periwinkle and the tough dog-fish
At even-tide have got into my dish.

The great, where are they now! the great had said—
This is not seemly! Bring to him instead
That which serves his and serves our dignity—
And that was done.

I am O'Rahilly!
Here in a distant place he holds his tongue,
Who once said all his say, when he was young!

The sureness of tone and feeling, the hard, concrete detail of
the language, the subtle weave of the rhymes through the
rhythms of the free verse patterns, the sense of completeness
achieved as the poem comes full circle, are all evidence of a poet
in total command of his material.

'The Wave of Cliona', based on what is considered O'Rahilly's
finest poem, is more ambitious, though not quite so successful.
The original has its occasion in the fact that O'Rahilly has
been forced to live in a barren place above the sea. He cannot
sleep with the beating of the waves. In the poet's almost neurotic
consciousness the wave takes on a whole cluster of symbolic
meanings : he sees it not only as an active agent in his persecution, but also a symbolic lament for his patrons, the MacCarthys,
and ironically a possible source of hope and help for Ireland
from abroad. Stephens attempts a *tour de force* in trying to
combine all of these themes with an effort to catch in words
the thunder of the sea, as in lines like these :

O Wave of Cliona, cease thy bellowing!
And let mine ears forget a while to ring
At thy long, lamentable misery . . .
Ease thee, cease thy long keening, cry no more.
End is, and here is end, and end is sore,
And to all lamentation be there end :
If I might come on thee, O howling friend!
Knowing that sails were drumming on the sea
Westward to Eire, and that help would be
Trampling for her upon a Spanish deck,
I'd ram thy lamentation down thy neck.

The ambition o'erleaps itself; the effect is perhaps too operatic. But its pounding energy is more effective than, for instance, Frank O'Connor's more literal rendering of the last four lines:

> Ah, famous wave you sang the livelong night below,
> Small wonder if the noise set my wits wandering—
> I swear if help could ever come to Ireland now
> I'd strangle in your raucous throat that song you sing.

A different aspect of O'Rahilly emerges in 'Eileen, Diarmuid and Teig'. Here the challenge is that of picking up a tone of quite exquisite tenderness and regret for the dead children, which O'Rahilly sustains throughout the second half of his long elegy. The result is one of Stephens's most perfect poems. The succession of metaphors in which the children's memory is celebrated is unified by a remarkable verbal texture wherein the Gaelic use of assonance is transferred with delicacy and tact to the English poem:

> Be kind unto these three, O King!
> For they were fragrant-skinned, cheerful, and giving!
>
> Three stainless pearls! Three of mild winning ways!
> Three candles sending forth three pleasant rays.
>
> Three vines! Three doves! Three apples on a bough!
> Three graces in a house. Three who refused nohow
>
> Help to the needy! Three of slenderness!
> Three memories for the companionless!
>
> Three strings of music! Three deep holes in clay!
> Three lovely children who loved Christ alway!
>
> Three mouths! Three hearts! Three minds beneath a
> stone;
> Ruin it is! Three causes for the moan
>
> That rises for three children dead and gone!
> Be kind, O King, unto this two and one!

As with 'Egan O'Rahilly' the first and last lines frame the experience; the opening and closing prayers complete the circuit and the rosary of separate metaphors is linked into unity.

Raftery and the Rhetoric of Love

In his note to *Reincarnations* Stephens records that 'a lover of
Raftery might not know I was indebted to this poet for my
songs.' With the one exception, 'The County Mayo', this is
so precise an admission that one is justified in treating the Raftery
material as original poetry. Those of them that appear in the
collected edition are 'Mary Hynes', 'The Coolin', the two poems
entitled 'Peggy Mitchell', 'Nancy Walsh', 'Anthony O'Daly',
'Mary Ruane', 'William O'Kelly', and 'The County Mayo' which
is a close translation. Most of them appear among the love
poems in Book II of *Collected Poems* entitled 'The Honey-
comb'.

A long letter which Stephens wrote to John Quinn in August
1917 describes his mood in writing these poems and his sense of
exhilaration at their success:

Here, by the way is one of the blessed little poems I wrote. I
nailed one line from the Irish of Raftery, and round that line
I blew a bubble of English verse, as follows:
>   She is the sky of the sun
>   She is the dart
>   Of love,
>   She is the love of my heart,
>   She is a rune,
>   She is above
>   The women of the race of Eve
>   As the sun is above the moon.

This first stanza of 'Mary Hynes'—the same 'peasant girl com-
mended by a song' mentioned in Yeats's 'The Tower'—is characteristic of the mood and method of these love poems. Most of
them are celebrations of female beauty, executed in a spirit of
delicate extravagance. Images and conceits that had been commonplace in the Irish originals are taken and charged with a
new energy and radiance in these short lyric flights. 'Nancy
Walsh' begins

>   It is not on her gown
>   She fears to tread;
>   But on her hair
>   That tumbles down

And strays
About her ways.

One notices, as with 'Mary Hynes', the manner in which the short lines as they move at their deliberate pace down the page insist on the precision and particularity of the images presented. 'The Coolin', perhaps the most perfect of these short love lyrics is shaped in regular stanzaic form and sustains a mood of stillness and intimacy in its evocation of the lover's night:

What if the night be black!
Or the air on the mountain chill!
Where the goat lies down in her track,
And all but the fern is still!

Stay with me under my coat!
And we will drink our fill
Of the milk of the white goat
Out on the side of the hill!

His one attempt at a close translation, 'The County Mayo', is one of the most successful and faithful renderings of this most famous of Raftery's lyrics, 'Cill Aodain'. His third stanza in particular captures the easy, vagrant grace of its original:

I say and swear that my heart lifts up like the lifting of a tide;
Rising up like the rising wind till fog or mist must go,
When I remember Carra, and Gallen close beside,
And the Gap of the Two Bushes, and the wide plains of Mayo.

As a volume *Reincarnations* marks a striking revival of Stephens's capacities as a poet. It lacks the complexity of thought, the sense of a spiritual search, which had marked *Insurrections* and more particularly *The Hill of Vision*. The material upon which the poet worked in the Gaelic poets was not intellectually demanding. The themes of poverty, patronage and love were already there. The challenge was in the finding of a language and technique to render them. The language of anger and complaint had already been discovered in the early dramatic lyrics. In *Reincarnations* that original colloquial style with its earthy idiom and concreteness of imagery is brought to a far higher degree of sophistication. Similarly the nature and love poetry of *Songs from the Clay* can be seen as paying rich dividends when Stephens encounters these concerns again in the lyrics of Raftery. What had been attempted in the English pastoral with borrowed diction and conventional imagery is now successfully achieved with a new economy and spareness. Finally the extended expedition into Ireland's past which *Reincarnations* involved gave Stephens a bridgehead on traditional Irish literature, and to that extent prepared the way for the mythological prose redactions which were to occupy the years immediately ahead.

9

Myth, Wonder-Tale and Epic

IRISH FAIRY TALES 1920
DEIRDRE 1923
IN THE LAND OF YOUTH 1924

The Modern Fashion

The idea of writing a collection of Irish fairy tales was first suggested to Stephens by his American friend, W. T. H. Howe as far back as 1913, and in a letter of that year Stephens responded favourably to the notion.[1] When he addressed himself to the project around 1918 larger possibilities began to present themselves. In November of that year he wrote to Pinker, his agent, in the following terms:

> In the matter of the tales which I have lately been sending you, however, they are easily the best things I have ever written, and the treatment, in each case, is so modern that modernity itself is put out of date by it. Forgive me if I brag a little. I have fallen on real treasure trove, from the story-teller's point of view; and I doubt if stories equal to those I have lately sent are being offered anywhere to editors. If, however, there is no market for them neither you nor I can help that.[2]

Of the stories he had sent Pinker, however, only one, 'Mongan's Frenzy', was to appear in *Irish Fairy Tales*. The other three, 'The Adventures of Nera', 'The Vision of Angus' and 'In the Beech-wood', were kept over and incorporated in the complex narrative structure of *In the Land of Youth* which is made up of *réamh-scéalta* or 'prefatory tales' to the Irish epic, the *Táin Bó Cuailgne*. It is probable that when he began work on these individual stories from the Táin sequence he saw the opportunity of re-telling the entire epic in his 'modern' style and idiom. By 1920 the enterprise was settled in his mind. In a letter of that year to his publisher, Sir Frederick Macmillan, he wrote:

> Although the subject is of vast antiquity I am handling it in the most direct and modern fashion. It will be in five volumes. Each volume will be a complete story in itself, and can be read by itself, but each will yet form an introduction to the volume which succeeds it . . . The first volume *In the Land of the Young* is completed. The second volume *Deirdre* is practically on its last chapter.[3]

As it turned out Stephens did not proceed with the task beyond the second volume. And in fact *Deirdre* was to appear in print a year before *In the Land of Youth*, as the second volume was eventually entitled. Because the latter work is closer in spirit and material to *Irish Fairy Tales* it is better discussed in the order of its writing rather than of its publication.

What Stephens meant by a 'modern' treatment of the old stories can only be inferred from the actual writing, and from the ways in which it differs from the work of his predecessors in the field. The most obvious models would have been Standish James O'Grady's Cuchulain narratives, Lady Gregory's *Cuchulain of Muirtheimne* and *Gods and Fighting Men*, and P. W. Joyce's *Old Celtic Romances*. O'Grady's renderings, though powerful in their way, are in a sonorous biblical style that seeks to infuse his epic personages with the maximum dignity and grandeur. As Ferguson had done in his poetic redactions O'Grady deliberately excludes the element of comic grotesquerie so frequent in the old tales and which Stephens plainly saw as one of their great attractions. Lady Gregory also eschews the comic grotesque but invests the narratives with a new homeliness in her racy Kiltartan dialect style. Joyce, as his Preface insists, emphasises the 'high and dignified tone and feeling' which he seems consistently to find in the originals, and attempts 'to render them in simple, plain, homely English'. Apart from these there were the various scholarly translations of the material, Eleanor Hull's edition of *The Cuchullin Saga*, Standish Hayes O'Grady's *Silva Gadelica* and A. H. Leahy's *Heroic Irish Romances*, all of which would have been available to Stephens in his task of creative redaction. Turning from these precedents one is struck by three features of

Stephens's artistic procedures that might reasonably be seen as modern and distinctive. These are the mystical treatment of vision, metamorphosis, re-incarnation and the afterlife; the cultivation of comic grotesquerie; the deliberate complexity of narrative structure which is even more notable in *In the Land of Youth* than in *The Demi-Gods*.

Myth and Mysticism

Yeats remarked in *Pages from a Diary* that 'James Stephens has read the Táin in the light of the Veda but the time is against him and he is silent.'[4] The comment, made in 1930, is supported by the fact that after the publication of *Reincarnations* Stephens's poetry had taken a decisive turn towards eastern mysticism. A number of these poems were published privately under the title *Little Things* in 1924. Among them was a poem entitled 'Nachiketas and Death' which he claimed had 'put the whole of the Upanishads & the Vedanta into verse'.[5] In 1918 AE had dedicated to Stephens his *Candle of Vision* which had as one of its overriding themes the mystical significance of the Celtic wonder-tales:

> That spiritual Overworld our Gaelic ancestors beheld was in essential the same as the Overworld revealed in the sacred books; and in the wonder tales of the Gael we find a great secular corroboration of sacred literature and of half-sacred philosophy such as Plato utters through the lips of Socrates. Earth, Mid-world, Heaven-world and the great deep of deity they knew as they are expounded in the Upanishads.[6]

Stephens, himself, had favourably reviewed James Cousins's book, *The Wisdom of the West*[7] in *The Irish Review* of 1912, and endorsed Cousins's thesis that the Irish mythological tales were a western account of Oriental mystical doctrines, adding to Cousins's conclusions the rather Jungian opinion that: 'Almost all the myths have for basis a trinity of persons typifying Consciousness, Energy and Matter; or Divinity, Soul and Body, and doing this they are all essays in experimental psychology.' The tales therefore that attract Stephens in the old Irish material are frequently concerned with reincarnation, metamorphosis and the different planes of being, and they are consistently rendered so as to draw out their universal rather than their local significance.

'The Story of Tuan Mac Cairill' which opens *Irish Fairy Tales* belongs to a type that scholars term the witness of antiquity. Like the lays of Oisin and Patrick it involves a conversation between a representative of paganism who has remained miraculously alive to recount ancient history and a saint. Though this aspect of the old tale is not neglected in Stephens's version the interest centres mainly on the stages of metamorphosis through which the hero, Tuan Mac Cairill goes as he witnesses the successive invasions of Ireland, as a stag, a boar, a hawk and finally as a salmon which is eventually caught, eaten by a queen and reborn into the world as a human child. It is in its empathetic descriptions of these animal sensations that Stephens's language is at its most strenuous : especially in such moments of intensity as when the salmon is hauled in a net from the water :

> I was in the air, and it was as though I were on fire. The air pressed on me like a fiery mountain. It beat on my scales and scorched them. It rushed down my throat and scalded me. It weighed on me and squeezed me, so that my eyes felt as though they must burst from my head, my head as though it would leap from my body, and my body as though it would swell and expand and fly in a thousand pieces.

What had been in the original story—at least in the eyes of its traditional readers—simply a device of witness, becomes for Stephens the focus of its interest and meaning and consequently the salient challenge to him as an artist in words.

A similar moment occurs in the Etain story of *In the Land of Youth* when the witch Fuamach, consumed with jealousy, invokes the help of the druid to transform the heroine into an insect and drive her onto another plane of being :

> 'Do what you tell yourself to do. Obey your desire. Fall, and fall and fall. Be winged. Be but a wing. Be lighter than the wind. Be but a living dust.'
>
> Agony ran through Etain's veins, and ecstasy ran with it in her mind. She willed to be that which she was commanded. She became a will; and, to the gigantic power working within her, she added all the strain and eagerness that was her own.
>
> She would be free. She would have wings. She would drop grossness. She would be lighter than the very rumour of the wind.

Her pale lips wrenched and gaped. Her eyes fixed. Her hands clenched and shook, and her brow of pearl gathered and knotted and froze.

Cousins, in his exegesis of the Etain story in *The Wisdom of the West*, represents Fuamach as 'the force projecting towards manifestation, the divine urge towards creation, symbolised as jealousy, driving out her rival from plane to plane . . . Creator of Karma, mistress of the Karmic winds'. This is the vision that Stephens imposes on the mythic tale, and the description of Etain's translation to a new plane is reminiscent of his mystical poems, especially 'The Breath of Life':

Infinite space was about her: swooning and infinite; infinite and giddy and swooning . . .
Before the eyes of Fuamach her body blinked suddenly. It blew out like a blown-out flame. It disappeared.

In the story of the two swineherds, Fruic and Rucht, who eventually become the two great bulls over whom the Táin conflict is fought, their successive metamorphoses are given the same energetic attention in Stephens's re-telling:

They began to change shapes then, thinking that in another form they might have a better chance; but they were always equal. One bit and the other tore, and the tear was as bad as the bite. They harried each other out of this shape and into that. They fought as birds, and in that shape they were known as Talon and Wing. Then they fought as sea-beasts and were called Shark and Whale. Then they became spectres called Shadow and Woe, and after that they were dragons. And in all these shapes they fought savagely.[8]

In two further stories from *Irish Fairy Tales* metamorphosis is the central theme, and both exhibit the author's peculiar ease at moving between different planes of reality. 'The Birth of Bran' relates with striking delicacy and humour how Fionn's two favourite dogs were half human, being born of a fairy princess while she was transformed by magic into a hound. 'Oisin's Mother', a sequel written in the same idiom, relates how Fionn's first wife, Saeve, came from the Shee in the form of a deer and was spared by Bran and Sceolan before turning into human

shape to become his wife. She was in the thrall of the Black
Magician of the Men of God who is again given the same Karmic
dimension that had invested Fuamach:

> 'His voice commands out of the spaces, and it demands secretly
> in the heart. He is not here or there, he is in all places at all
> times. I cannot escape from him,' she said, 'and I am afraid,'
> and at that she wept noiselessly and stared on Fionn.

There were two versions of the Otherworld in the ancient
Irish sagas: there were islands beyond the sea, variously called
Tir na n-Og—the Land of Youth—, the Many-coloured Land,
the Land of Wonder and the Land of Promise; there was the
Shee, fairy-mounds beneath the earth to which the Tuatha de
Danaan had withdrawn after the coming of the Gaels. The two
supernatural regions are not very sharply distinguished in the
mythological tales.[9] Stephens, having perhaps in mind the
Theosophist notion of the seven planes of existence already in-
voked in *The Demi-Gods*, imposed his own scheme on the Celtic
Otherworlds. At the opening of one of his finest stories, 'Becuma
of the White Skin', he outlines his conception thus:

> After this Earth there is the world of the Shi. Beyond it again
> lies the Many-Coloured Land. Next comes the Land of Won-
> der, and after that the Land of Promise awaits us. You will
> cross clay to get to the Shi; you will cross water to attain the
> Many-Coloured Land; fire must be passed ere the Land of
> Wonder is attained, but we do not know what will be crossed
> for the fourth world.

There is no warrant for this formula in the original tale.[10] But it
is invoked again and refined in *In the Land of Youth* where
Nera's fairy lover informs him:

> 'This world is called Tir na n-Og, the Land of the Young.
> It is within the world you have left, as an apple is within its
> skin, and all who die in your world come to this one. But
> within this world there is another called the Land of Wonders,
> and those who die here, or who can wish to do so, go to the
> Land of Wonders. Within the Land of Wonders there is yet a
> world called the Land of Promise, and those who die in the
> Land of Wonders are born into the Land of Promise, but they
> cannot die there until they can wish to do so.'

'And after the Land of Promise?'

'After the Land of Promise there is your world again.'

In Theosophical terms man occupies the fourth round of existence : in Stephens's second model of the Otherworld, therefore,
the three stages beyond earth outlined by Nera's lover would
correspond to the three Theosophist spheres above the human.
The imposition of this schema on the saga material seems to
spring from artistic rather than doctrinal impulses. As has been
seen in his early fantasies Stephens's tendency has always been
mythic and visionary, consistently impatient of the purely em-
pirical view of reality. Behind the world of mere sense experience
he insists on throwing the reflections of a spiritual world beyond,
on bringing the 'country of the gods' into creative relation with
the quotidian world of men. The Irish sagas presented him with
a landscape where gods and men constantly met and inter-
mingled, in which shapes were constantly changing and in which
one world constantly opened on the next. As it was a region of
experience that he determined to explore in an extensive way,
over six projected volumes, it was artistically imperative that he
should impose a unity on the far-flung and often fragmentary
matter offered by the old tales; that he should fix its co-ordinates
in time and space. Having done this he was at liberty to develop
those aspects of the material that most attracted his creative
gifts : its sense of the marvellous and grotesque, its often dazzling
evocation of an idyllic age of innocence, its vivid presentation of
love, war and magic, its casual transitions between different
planes of reality. It thus becomes his opportunity of exploring the
theme that most exercised him : the different conditions in which
the human soul may find itself, what he called in 'Becuma of the
White Skin' the 'gusty passage of world within world'.

Tale Within Tale

Already in *Irish Fairy Tales* there are foreshadowings of the
complex narrative pattern, the tale within tale, that makes *In the
Land of Youth* Stephens's most involuted fiction. The first and
last stories in the book are framed within the story of Saint
Finnian who acts as listener, interlocutor and recorder, and in
their turn they provide a frame for the collection. Furthermore
the last story, 'Mongan's Frenzy', employs two internal narrators,

Cairidé who tells the main story to the saint, and Mongan who relates a story within that story. 'Mongan's Frenzy' looks forward to the novel also in its use of three worlds, the christian, the pagan and the Shee, and two time-scales, the earthly and the supernatural. Within the temporal scheme of Stephens's world a day on earth is the equivalent of a minute in Faery. The disparity had already been invoked in another of the Fairy Tales, 'The Wooing of Becfola', and it is consistently exploited in the narrative method of *In the Land of Youth* to weave its component tales into a unified structure. This organisation of tale within tale and world within world has already driven critics to desperate straits for a language to describe it, so that Lloyd Frankenberger in the Introduction to his *Selection* calls it 'the nest-of-translucent-boxes technique' and again characterises it as a 'Geometry of the Translucently Faceted Dimensions of Timescape'. It is not only an infinitely reflexive narrational method, it is also a method by which the reader is never permitted for long to suspend his disbelief that what he is reading is fiction : continually he is startled by a casual shift from one world to the next, from one narrator to the next, one story to the next. As if in a mime of the imagination in reverie, the mind is led down an infinite regression of dream, wish, desire, fantasy, vision. The archetypal patterns of character and situation, the interplay of the primary emotions of love, pride, jealousy, anger, vengeance and warrior vainglory are so driven beyond the conventions of realism that they become radiated by a more quintessential sense of reality. So that one can perhaps relate them to Stephens's remark already quoted that myths 'are all essays in experimental psychology'. And one can assent to Lloyd Frankenberger's comment that 'In these clashings, some real, some phantasmal, between legendary, sometimes multiple, personalities a most curious transformation comes to pass. Realms, like subconscious, id, superego, ego are made bewilderingly simple.'

In the Land of Youth

In the Land of Youth is divided into two parts entitled 'The Feast of Samhain' and 'The Feast of Lugnasa'. During these two festivals of the Celtic year the gates of the Shee are traditionally open and movement is possible between the two worlds. The scene at the opening of both narratives is Maeve's court at

Cruachan in Connacht which remains the hub at the centre of the narrative wheels which make up the book's action. Fergus and his Ulstermen are present, indicating that, in terms of the time sequence of the Táin, the Deirdre story is over—it had been the occasion for Fergus's defection to Connacht. Yet most of the book's action deals with a time previous to that event.

The three narratives that make up 'The Feast of Lugnasa' are listed by Eleanor Hull in her *Cuchullin Saga*[11] as Prefatory Tales to the Táin. Only one of them, the visit of Nera to the Otherworld and his return, is related directly by the author. Nera accepts the challenge of Ailill—Maeve's husband—to go out to the hill of execution and tie a withy round the foot of a man hanged there. On his return he sees what he thinks is the slaughter of Ailill and his court at the hands of Ethal Anbual, ruler of the Connacht Shee, and he follows the retreating invaders into the Otherworld. There he lives for three days an idyllic life with a woman of the Shee from whom he learns that the assault on Cruachan had been merely a rehearsal for the real attack which has been planned for the following Samhain. He is further told that his three days have been three minutes of earthly time. He is therefore enabled to return to Cruachan to claim a prize for his bravery and to warn his companions of the planned attack before returning to his fairy lover. He remains long enough to hear the second story, the Vision of Angus, which is related by Maeve. This story provides the explanation for Ethal Anbual's enmity towards Maeve—she had sacked his Shee to secure his daughter Caer, as a wife for Angus Og. The third story, that of the Dispute of the Two Swineherds, is, in turn, inset in the middle of Maeve's narrative. It is related by Bove—King of the Shee of Femen—to the Dagda and his company when they visit him for help in finding the object of Angus's visionary desire, Caer. It is the story referred to earlier about the two swineherds who become metamorphosed into the two bulls, and thus become the cause of the war between Connacht and Ulster in the central action of the Táin. 'The Feast of Lugnasa' begins and ends in the banqueting hall at Cruachan, and its framing story is of one night's duration. But it takes the reader's mind through several time-scales and a variety of narrative morphologies, romantic, epic, comic, tragic, grotesque. The sinister darkness that surrounds Cruachan as the story opens and closes is merely the outer shell around other worlds of light and radiance. And the reader's access to these is through the imagination of Maeve and of Bove, the magical perspectives thrown open by their narrative prowess. The progress of the reader's attention is from the epic, human world of the banqueting, story-telling and war, then to the Faery world with its sunlit transparencies, its quintessential desires and visions, and then further to the aboriginal and grotesque patterns of the swineherds' narrative, the insatiable pigs, the metamorphoses, the relentless cycle of their warfare. Thus the art of the story-teller, of Stephens and his fictional agents, becomes the visionary process by which successive layers of existential reality are stripped away and world within world revealed.

Though each of these worlds parallels the others in the manner outlined by Nera's fairy mistress, each has a different mode or fabric of thought and action. Nera, though lyrically happy in the Shee of Connacht, retains his warrior longing for the sword that Ailill had promised him as a prize for his exploit on the hill of the hanged men. Despite her admonitions to him about inordinate desire he cannot extinguish his wish for the earthly reward :

'I see that it is of no use to wish at all,' cried Nera discontentedly.

'Yes,' she replied, 'you may desire things which everybody can enjoy with you, and that is true wishing.'

'Such things as—?'

'Sunlight and the song of birds, good food and health, a contented mind and a good understanding. These hurt no one and every one is better for possessing them, or for living among people who have them.'

Nera revolved these thoughts, but it seemed to him that they were not profitable, for he considered that the things worth having were those which other people lacked, and he thought there was very small value in possessions that anybody might enjoy who cared to want them.

It is this incorrigible tendency in the human to desire what properly belongs to others that gives force and liveliness to the turbulent, untidy mortal world at the court of Cruachan, and that lies at the root of the book's specifically epic action, even the Táin itself. It is also one of the many human tendencies which the gods are willing to exploit for their own purposes. Thus in Maeve's story of the vision of Angus, the Dagda, having discovered the identity and location of Caer, realises that he cannot invade the Shee to obtain her for his son :

'Have you a suggestion to make?' said the Dagda.
'I have one,' Bove interposed.
'Make it,' said the Dagda.
'It would be very wrong for us to do a thing that was wrong,' said Bove, 'and, therefore, we shall not do it.'
'We certainly shall not,' Fergne agreed.
'But there are other people, and it is right for those people to do what is wrong.'
'How so?' said Fergne, scandalised.
'Wrongdoing is their base of existence,' said Bove.
'What people are those?' the Dagda inquired.
'Mortals,' Bove replied.

When they approach Maeve with their proposition she is easily persuaded: she sacks the Shee of Connacht and takes back not only Caer but the two bulls which are to be cause of the Táin conflict.

'The Feast of Lugnasa', though it covers a thousand years of earthly time, and involves the successive metempsychosis of the heroine, Etain, from fairy woman, to insect, to human princess and finally to swan, its narrative pattern, involving as it does no other story, is comparatively uncomplicated. It too is related by Maeve at the Cruachan court to the same company which had been assembled there on the feast of Samhain. Its relation to the Táin story is less obvious than were the three stories that made up the book's first part : in *The Cuchullin Saga* it is included among the 'Miscellaneous Tales Connected with the Saga'. If Stephens had completed his plan for five volumes we would be better able to judge what part he had in mind for the Etain's story within the epic enterprise. But because of its nature the story had an obvious intrinsic interest for him. And the manner in which he dramatises the Etain's three love affairs— with Angus, Eochaidh and Midir—her inner conflicts, the intensities of anguish she suffered in being translated from one psychic condition to the next and the power struggle between her earthly and fairy lovers makes it one of Stephens's most impressive fictional achievements.

The Comic Grotesque

There is a quality in traditional Irish story-telling that seems to perplex the translator while providing a comic opportunity for the deliberate parodist. This is the frequency of the conventional epithet, the epic simile and the accumulation of sonorous adjectives in the set pieces. Joyce exploits these verbal patterns for his satiric purposes in the Cyclops episode of *Ulysses,* and later Flann O'Brien exploits them to achieve effects of multiple absurdity in the Finn Mac Cool passages of his experimental novel, *At Swim Two Birds.* Even in scholarly translation these verbal sequences can strike a modern reader as almost deliberately humorous. A comparison of a passage from Standish H. O'Grady's scrupulous translation of 'Bruidhen Bheg na hAlmaine' with the same passage as rendered by Stephens in 'The Little Brawl of Allen' throws an interesting light on the topic. The brawl that breaks out between the warriors of Fionn and of Goll at the royal palace occurs in the middle of a feast and is described with epic gusto. In the midst of it this passage appears:

> An ill place it had been for a feeble invalid, or delicate taper-fingered woman, or aged senior of long date, to be in; the little brawl of Allen on that night, a-listening to groans of young and old, of high and low, as they lay maimed, faint and infirm, or were stricken down and cut up. (O'Grady)[12]

> That was no place for a sick person to be. It was not a corner which a slender-fingered woman would choose to do up her hair; nor was it a spot an ancient man would choose to think quietly in, for the tumult of sword on sword, of axe on shield, the roar of the contending parties, the crying of wounded men, and the screaming of frightened women destroyed peace, and over all was the rallying cry of Goll Mac Morna and the great shout of Fionn. (Stephens)

The O'Grady version is droll, as it were, by accident: the conventional epithet 'taper-fingered', a precise translation of the original 'mhéirlebair', is unavoidably eccentric in English. Stephens seizes on the oddity and makes it a deliberate device of extravagant inconsequentiality: the slender-fingered woman is now presented as doing up her hair, the ancient man as wanting a place to think quietly. The Gaelic convention is thus exaggerated to the point at which it enacts a humorous parody on itself.

In the sensations of the salmon being torn from its element in 'The Story of Tuan Mac Cairill' and in the transformation of Etain into an insect, one saw Stephens's concern with intensities of feeling and his coercing of language to register these intensities. This tendency is equally strenuous in his comic situations. The action of 'The Carl of the Drab Coat' concentrates on two human activities, running and watching. Thus the two protagonists, the Carl and Cael, become grotesque embodiments of their exertion :

> 'If you won't try to run, my treasure,' said the Carl, 'you will never get your tribute.'
> And with that he incensed and exploded himself into an eye-blinding, continuous waggle and complexity of boots, that left Cael behind him in a flash.
> 'I will run until I burst,' sobbed Cael, and he screwed agitation and despair into his legs until he hummed and buzzed like a blue-bottle on a window.

Fionn and his watchers on Ben Edair accordingly become distilled to the one human feeling of watchful expectancy :

> 'Look again,' said Fionn.
> The eagle-eyed man lifted a face, thin and sharp as though it had been carven on the wind, and he stared forward with an immobile intentness.
> 'What do you see?' said Fionn.
> 'Nothing,' the man replied.
> 'I will look myself,' said Fionn, and his great brow bent forward and gloomed afar.
> The watcher stood beside, staring with his tense face and unwinking, lidless eye.
> 'What can you see, O Fionn?' said the watcher.
> 'I can see nothing,' said Fionn, and he projected again his grim gaunt forehead. For it seemed as if the watcher stared with his whole face, ay, and with his hands; but Fionn brooded weightedly on distance with his puckered and crannied brow.

And when the watcher gets his first tentative glimpse of what might be the runners he becomes 'an eye, a rigidity, an intense out-thrusting and ransacking of thin-spun distance.'

In the story of the two swineherds the Munster pigs become an exorbitant parody of fatness, while the Connacht pig is presented as a caricature of thinness and hunger :

> He became gaunt as a winter wolf and spiny as a hedgehog.
> His skull stuck out, lean as a hatchet and pointed as a spear.
> His legs grew as lanky as a young foal's, and his upper anatomy was all chest and no stomach like a coursing hound.
> His tail poked outwards and downwards like a piece of wet string pasted on a bone.

As hunger possesses the Connacht swine, the resources of Stephens's language are called up to embody its grotesque extremity :

> Their hunger was such that they screamed from the rage of it, and the air whistled through their long lean snouts like the whistle of a wintry gale through a hole.
> There were no people left in Munster but the deaf men, and they recovered their hearing; that is, they had hearing thrust violently upon them, and they cursed the gift as they fled.[13]

The world through which we move in these two books is one of prodigies, where the movements of the mind and the body are rehearsed on a level of radical intensity : the landscape is always either exquisitely vernal and radiant or profoundly threatening; love, rage, jealousy or desire, freed from the inhibitions of realism, find expression as imagined distillations of their earthly forms; the heroes, be they runners, fighters, statesmen or magicians, act and move as if moved by a single impulse, that of their calling; the monsters—hogs, giant toads, venomous dogs and sheep—are inordinately yet convincingly monstrous. The strength of the writing resides in its sustained fidelity to this imagined landscape and in its consistent power to draw the reader's mind into this world that is at such a remove from the quotidian, yet which enacts a drama uncannily relevant to the inner workings of the human consciousness in its interludes of dream, nightmare and reverie. It is this quality that makes these two books so strikingly different from any other attempt to re-tell the Irish sagas in modern prose.

Epic as Fiction

The Deirdre legend has held a long-standing and continuing fascination for creative writers because of its inherently dramatic qualities which recall both the story of Helen and that of Isolde. Prior to Stephens's *Deirdre* Ferguson, Yeats, AE and Synge had already re-worked the material as theatre. Stephens was the first, and is so far the only writer to adapt it to the novel form. *In the Land of Youth* is not a novel: in common with the mythic and epic material that it re-shapes it is not deeply concerned with the careful examination of character and motive; the personages and their motives are taken for granted—wherever it is not managed by magical agencies—and the emphasis is on their actions. In *Deirdre* Stephens faces the challenge—not encountered to any great extent in the theatre—of building up an elaborate social world and of supplying a consistent web of psychological motivations for the characters who move within it. The way in which Stephens sets about the task throws valuable light on his procedures throughout the novel.

There is a formidable improbability at the opening of the tale in both its original versions. The story opens in the house of Felimid: Conachur, the king, Cathfa, the druid, and Bricriu, the mocker, are present. Felimid's wife is pregnant and in the hearing of the warriors the child cries out in her womb. Called upon to explain the phenomenon Cathfa declares that a woman child is to be born, that her name will be Deirdre, and that she will bring destruction on Ulster.[14]

> 'Let that maiden be slain!' cried out the young men of Ulster.
> 'Not so!' said Conchubar; 'let her in the morning be brought to me, and she shall be reared according to my will, and she shall be my wife, and in my companionship shall she be.'
> The men of Ulster were not so hardy as to turn him from his purpose, and thus it was done.

This is the idiom of epic. A novel cannot afford to be so cryptic and perfunctory. The novelist must convey why the king decided to defy at once his warriors and the prophecy, and how he hoped that making Deirdre his queen would neutralise rather than increase her threat to his kingdom. Stephens's handling of the incident in his first chapter exemplifies the difference between the two modes:

> They carried the little morsel to him and she was laid across his knees.
>
> 'So you are to destroy my kingdom and bring evil to mighty Ireland?'
>
> The babe reached with a tiny claw and gripped one finger of the King.
>
> 'See,' he laughed, 'she places herself under my protection,' and he moved his finger to and fro but the child held fast to it.
>
> 'Ulster is under your protection,' growled Bricriu. The King, who did not like other men's advice, looked at him.
>
> 'It is not soldierly, nor the act of a prince to evade fate,' said he who was to be known afterwards as the wide-eyed, majestic monarch. 'Therefore, all that can happen will happen, and we shall bear all that is to be borne.'
>
> Then he gave the child back to its trembling nurse.
>
> Cathfa looked up from the chess-board.
>
> 'She is to be called the "Troubler",' said he.
>
> And from that day 'Deirdre' was her name.

We are here in the world of fiction. The grip of the child's hand is a novelist's device as is Conachur's stern reaction to the rebuke of Bricriu. The characters of both are revealed in the incident: Bricriu is sharp, witty and astringent in preparation for his sinister role in the projected Táin sequence; Conachur is proud, moody and headstrong. There is a well-pointed irony in his invocation of fate, as it is fate and the grim working out of the prophecy that finally crush him. Most significantly there is no mention of Deirdre being brought up to be his wife. This idea is suggested to Conachur by the nurse, Lavarcham, at the end of Chapter VII when Deirdre has reached the age of sixteen. By this time the king has been forsaken by his former wife, Maeve, and is in search of a new queen. When, in Chapter XVIII, he sees Deirdre for the first time he falls in love with her and demands importunately to marry her within the week. There is no reference to the prophecy. The primitive contour of the epic is thus modified and domesticated to the psychological and social motivations of the novel.

Similarly when handling the elements of magic, clairvoyance and ritual taboo, available in the old story and largely inseparable from its movement, Stephens subordinates them to the fictional mode. In one version of the original legend Deirdre, during the Scottish exile, sees in vision three birds who come with honey in their bills and depart with blood. In the novel this, and subsequent visions, come to her in dreams. When the three brothers arrive with Deirdre in Ireland under the protection of Fergus, the sea-chieftain Borach invites Fergus to a feast which Fergus is under *geasa*, or taboo, not to refuse. In the Irish version Borach has no personality, he is a mere functionary in the action. In Stephens's version, however, his character has been built up in the previous chapters sufficiently to charge the incident with psychological tension :

> He looked with his black, deep-set peep at Deirdre and kissed her, but when she looked at him he turned aside.
>
> He was ill at ease, and all his movements were self-conscious and unhappy. He turned, almost truculently, to Fergus.
>
> 'Fergus,' he said, 'I am honoured to see you in my lordship.'
>
> 'You are kind,' said Fergus, 'and I shall bind you to visit me in mine.'
>
> 'I am so delighted', Borach continued hastily, 'that I have prepared a feast for you, such as is only offered to a king.'

And when, in the last chapter but one, Deirdre and her companions are overwhelmed in the magic sea thrown about them by the druid, Cathfa, the action is presented from within the minds of the victims :

> Naoise dropped on one knee, rose again, leaped high in the air, and dropped on his knee. Deirdre fell to the ground and rose up gasping. Ardan rolled over on his back, tossed his shield away, and came slowly up again, beating the air with his hands. Ainnle went half-way down, rose again, and continued his advance on tip-toe.
>
> A look of dismay and rage came on Naoise's face. He moved with extraordinary slowness to Deirdre and lifted her to his shoulder.

'We are lost,' he said. 'That Magician!'

'Keep on swimming,' Ardan giggled. 'There was never water here before, but the whole sea has risen around our legs, and we may paddle to Uisneac.'

The manner of their defeat gives a perfect symmetry to the fable: Cathfa who had at the outset foretold the fate of Deirdre is thus the instrument by which his prophecy is finally fulfilled.

The Drama of Jealousy

The action of *Deirdre* is uncannily similar to that of *The Char-woman's Daughter*. In the earlier novel the heroine—like Caitilin in *The Crock of Gold* and Mary MacCann in *The Demi-Gods* —is on the brink of womanhood. She is appropriated by an older man, a figure of power and possessiveness. When she escapes from him she is pursued by his ineradicable anger and jealousy. In each case there is a possessive mother figure—Mrs Make-believe, Lavarcham—who tries not only to protect her but to live again through her. The contrast between the heroine and her elder suitor in the early and middle phases of both novels is strongly marked. Mary was 'almost mesmerised by the huge, tweed-clad legs that towered like monoliths beside her'. When Deirdre is first introduced to Conachur—'She arose and stood with downcast eyes. She did not dare to look at him. All that came within her vision was a mighty leg draped in green silk, from which long tassels of gold swung gently.' Conachur falls in love with her and, confident of his power, assumes that he can possess her. But just as Mary had been abashed by the 'god-like' massiveness of the Policeman, Deirdre cannot conceive the possibility of loving the king on equal terms: 'Nothing but terror filled her heart at that prospect, for she could not see him in any terms of intimacy or affection. . . . He was like some god that had come out of the hills to astonish and terrify.' Her love for Naoise, on the other hand, is another version of Mary's affection for the young clerk: 'The youth who was hers! Who had no terrors for her! Who was her equal in years and frolic! She could laugh with him, and at him. She could chide him and love him. She could give to him and withhold. She could be his mother as well as his wife.' Lavarcham differs from the charwoman only in her superior subtlety. She is possessed by her ambition to make Deirdre queen and even Conachur yields to her ferocity when she insists that he must not take Deirdre before the wedding ceremony. But even when she fails in her ambition and is deceived—by Deirdre's eloping with Naoise—she continues to work for her protegée in covert defiance of the King's will.

The drama of sexual jealousy is the most persistent theme in Stephens's fiction. It is obviously allied to the theme of male and female opposition which had already found expression both in his poetry and in his various fictions. It receives its most concentrated expression in the phantasmagoric tale, 'Etched in Moonlight' which, perhaps significantly, appeared in three successive issues of *The Dublin Magazine* in 1923, the year in which *Deirdre* was published. The action and structure of *Deirdre* turns on Conachur's jealousy. Though the book's omniscient point of view gives us continual access to the thoughts of the other characters —the love passion of Deirdre and Naoise, the contrivances of Lavarcham, the vacillations of Fergus—it is the jealous torment of Conachur that dominates its process. The occasion of the Deirdre story is the latter's failure with Maeve whose defection inflicts on him a humiliation which he finds hard to conceal. The Maeve incident does not properly belong to the original story of the Sons of Uisneac. It was imported for a double purpose. Stephens had to keep in mind his larger plan to re-tell the entire Táin in which Maeve is a crucial element. She is therefore present and prominent in the first two volumes. And Stephens, conscious of the demands of the novel form, needed a means of establishing Conachur's character before bringing it to bear on the drama of the central tale. Roger McHugh is clearly right in suggesting that the Maeve incident supplies Conachur 'with an additional motive for revenge. . . . His thwarted rage comes back with additional fury, when in years later, Conachur is cheated of a second woman, Deirdre.'[15]

In Stephens's account Conachur is doomed to be as great a failure in love as he is destined to be a success in war and administration. The novel begins as a comedy, and ends as a tragedy, of sexual relationships. On the first page Conachur, in the house of Felimid, sends a message to his host that 'his wife is to sleep with me tonight'. And he receives his first reversal because the wife is in the last stage of childbirth, and the child in question is Deirdre. When told that the arrangement is impossible he remarks moodily that 'These women are always troublesome,' and the irony of that comment is to resonate through the ensuing action. In his affair with Maeve, Conachur proved equally maladroit. We learn that 'matrimony had been poisoned for them at the very fountain, and a dear, detestable memory for Maeve was that her husband had outraged her before he married her, and that he had taken her then and there-after in her own despite'.[16] His sexual indelicacy is further em-phasised in the otherwise gratuitous dialogue between him and Lavarcham in Chapter II of Book IV. There he describes rue-fully how he insisted on his seigneurial rights over Cuchullin's wife, Emer, rights which were only conceded on condition that Fergus spent the night in the same bed with them. As we have seen he is determined to take Deirdre before the wedding night and is only deflected by Lavarcham's even greater determination : 'If I bring her my knife will be in her bosom.'

From the moment that the elopement becomes public the psychological drama is in the mind of the king, and as Book I ends he is, as it were, at the centre of the stage :

> A whisper, a thrill, a terrible constriction of the heart fled through the vast palace, and went zig-zagging like wildfire about Ulster. And in the centre of that Conachur stood, alone; and his fists closed and his eyes closed; listening to the whis-pers that were an inch away and a hundred miles away, that were over him and under him and in him; listening to the blanching of his face and the liquefying of his bones; listening in a rage of curiosity and woe for the more that might be said and all the more that might be thought; trying, as with one gripping of the mind, to sense all the bitterness that might be, to exhaust it in one gulp, and re-awaken as at a million removes from all that had ever been or could be till doom.

The internal drama of jealousy and thwarted pride evinced here broods over the second book of the novel and throws an ominous shadow over the action even when it moves from Conachur's court. The working out of Cathfa's prophecy now becomes the working out of the king's jealous obsession through a pattern of vengeance. When he announces his forgiveness of the fugitives, and his desire for their return and rehabilitation, the courtiers are relieved and delighted, but the reader is seldom in doubt as to his darker purposes. The four are doomed on their level as surely as he is spiritually desolated on his.

Consequently as the story draws towards its culmination Conachur is the primary focus of interest. The defence of the Red Branch by the four fugitives and the two sons of Fergus is, in its way, a marvellous *tour de force*. Always the most careful of writers, Stephens works out an elaborate strategy of battle for the defenders and describes the fighting with a remarkable technical vividness and precision. But it is the spiritual devastation of Conachur that gives these final chapters their force. Deserted by the chivalry of Ulster, he must depend on his jabbering and demoralised mercenaries to do his fighting. His obsession has drained him of his virtue and almost of his dignity. He waits for the 'spectral apparition of dawn':

> A harsh, grey, iron-bound upper-world brooded on a chill and wrinkled earth. The king's eyes and the eyes of his captain scanned each other from colourless, bleak faces. There was no hue in their garments; their shields were dull as death; and their hands, each clutching a weapon, seemed like the knotted claws of goblins.
>
> A slow, sad exhalation came from the king's grey lips, like the plaint of some grim merman of the sea, rising away and alone amid the chop and shudder of dismal waters.

In this sense the book might have more appropriately taken its title from Conachur. It is he that dominates the beginning and the end, and it is the momentum of his obsessive jealousy that carries the action through its chief intermediary phases. The drama of sexual jealousy, the tension between love and power that works itself out in his psyche, were plainly the elements in the Deirdre story that attracted and sustained Stephens's creative attention.

What stands out most clearly from a survey of these three mythological fictions is their remarkable originality and their relentless experimentation with form, language and narrative techniques. At no stage do we get the impression of an author writing to a programme or working to a preordained fictional formula. Each successive story is encountered as a particular and unique challenge to the shaping and transforming imagination.

Of the three, *In the Land of Youth* is the most individual and vivid by virtue of its elaborate and delicate intricacy, its curious fusion of form and subject matter. By comparison, *Deirdre*, though by no means commonplace, is conventional in its linear plot and traditional handling of character and motive. Of the *Irish Fairy Tales*, the opening story of Tuan Mac Cairill, the author's own favourite, is perhaps the most remarkable for its unusual agility and intensity of language.

Why Stephens abandoned the Táin after two such successful volumes has never been satisfactorily explained. It may have been because the books had not been a great commercial success, though *Deirdre* had won the Tailtean Prize for literature in 1924. It may have been that in Yeats's phrase the time was against him : the Black and Tan War and the Civil War that followed it did a great deal to destroy the enthusiasm for heroic Irish romance. The fact that he removed to England in January of 1924 may also have been relevant : away from the Dublin libraries and the atmosphere of Celtic scholarship in which he had moved, the enterprise became for him more difficult and perhaps less beguiling. In any case his removal to London marked a sharp decline in his literary output. From that point until his death in 1950 his only new creative work consisted of two volumes of poetry and one chapter of an autobiography which he never completed. It was therefore fortunate that he had conceived of his first two heroic romances as self-sustaining works and to that extent as independent of the larger epic enterprise.

Theme and Variations

COLLECTED POEMS, 1926
STRICT JOY, 1931
KINGS AND THE MOON, 1938

Unutterable Transcendency

Stephens's poetry after *Reincarnations* is overtly mystical. That is to say that its theme and focus are transcendentalist. It rarely concerns itself with the material or social world, with people or with nature. Rather it seeks to define and celebrate the Absolute, the Vedantic version of the deity, the source of all reality, which is itself unknowable and unutterable. The principle of godhead is variously named the Absolute, the Will, the Demiurge, the breath of life or simply 'That'. In a letter to Stephen MacKenna probably written in 1927 Stephens makes clear that the personal or anthropomorphic deity of the early poetry is no longer viable at any level of apprehension:

> ... if you tackle me on the Veda I'll uphold to the death that the 'great sentences' are true, or are nothing, & that the greatest of the great sentences 'Thou Art That' is exactly so and thus. Thank all the goodnesses there is no God in the Vedanta —There is a That, and I feel natively capable of being a That where I should hesitate long & shrink from the possibility of being a child of God. Anyone can be and enjoy being a That: and every Relative can tumble to his Absolute in the twinkling of an eye, as it were. Observe that in the Vedas every statement that can possibly be made is qualified by the words 'as it were'. I like the Vedanta, & I don't like Christianity.[1]

This position was already explicit in one of the last poems of *The Hill of Vision*, 'The Breath of Life', and the poet's reading

throughout the intervening decade buttressed and deepened it. Its
corollary for a poet as deeply religious as Stephens is that the
material world, which now appears 'but a dream / In vacancy,
dreamed by the conjuror,'[2] ceases to be a proper object of the
poet's attention.

In poetic terms this change of outlook and emphasis presents
Stephens with an almost insoluble problem : the supreme object
of his poetry is no longer amenable to language. His deity has
no attributes and is therefore inexpressible. The ecstatic experience of union between the human soul and the Absolute is by
definition a self-emptying process whose final aim is 'nothingness'.
The material world is at worst an illusion, at best a source of
metaphors for a poetic enterprise that sets out under heavy
handicap. In the face of these difficulties the poet is reduced to
finding successive formulations for his mystical doctrine and to
reiterated assertions of its truth. The truth can only be asserted,
it cannot be poetically dramatised. And the assertion itself must
proceed by means of approximations, obliquities and negations,
as in the final stanza of 'The Crest Jewel' where he claims to raise
the accepted doctrine of the soul to 'an absolute utterance' :[3]

> It has been writ in wisdom old—
> This is the last word to be told :
>
> There is no dissolution ! No
> Creation ! There is no woe !
>
> There is no teacher, teaching, taught !
> Are none who long for, lack for aught !
>
> Are none who pine for freedom ! None
> Are Liberated under sun !
>
> —And this absolutely true
> In Him who dreams in me and you.[4]

Only the Vedantic initiate can hope to receive such writing as
poetry or even as truth. It is versified doctrine unconcerned with
enacting or manifesting its validity; unless the reader is altogether
obedient to 'wisdom old' it is hard to see how he can be persuaded.

In 1922 Stephens wrote excitedly to his American friend,
Howe, that he had managed to put 'the whole of the Upanishads

F

& the Vedanta into verse'.[5] The poem in question, 'Nachiketas and Death',[6] reveals an attitude to poetry similar to that evinced in 'The Crest Jewel'. He seems content to gloss and expound a body of doctrine to which he has already given spiritual assent, and from which the drama of discovery and argument has already departed. The drama that remains is the manipulation of paradox in the service of an incorrigibly elusive world-view:

> No heaven, nor earth, nor middle part,
> There is no day or night;
> There is no beauty, truth, or wit,
> But That alone! And Thou Art It!

The transcendentalism of Emerson's 'Hymn to Brahma' and its unmistakable rhythms appear in a stanza that follows:

> He is the Dreamer, and the Dream!
> He is the Frightened, and the Fear!
> He is the Hope! the Gloom! the Gleam!
> He is the Season, and the Year!
> —He is not This, nor That, nor Yon:
> He is Thyself! And Thou Art One!

The lack of intellectual tension and the virtual absence of imagery are probably the cause for so much artificial emphasis —the capital letters, the exclamation marks, the archaisms. Without these devices his ballet of abstract nouns and pronouns around the copula would be intolerably flat.

Stephens finds himself, therefore, in a difficulty which confronts all mystical poets—that of expressing the inexpressible. He is furthermore in the predicament of the devotional poet which is that of finding a language which can convey fervour and reverence without falling into the cliché of prayer. But whereas Crashaw had his ensemble of saints and Hopkins the world's body Stephens has no human or material *dramatis personae*. He is therefore thrown on the hackneyed language of religion with its ceremonial archaisms and conventional verbal gestures of adoration; hence the recurrence of words like glory, splendour, bliss, loveliness, love, goodness, power, effulgence, ecstasy, wonder, and their various morphemes. Being mostly conceptual these words have no visual impact; and they have done such long service in ritual and worship that they have lost all freshness and particularity. Used in conjunction with concrete diction they are of course still viable, as a poet like Yeats never ceases to demonstrate. But when Stephens releases them onto the page, often in little singing groups, the effect is not even that of passable verse:

> Courage, goodness, tenderness:
> Wisdom, beauty, ecstasy:
> Wonder, love and loveliness:
> Hope and immortality:
>
> What is pure, or what is lovely?
> Nothing is that will endure![7]

Austin Clarke observed in Stephens's poetry a propensity which becomes especially marked in these later volumes, his use of 'a limited range of short substantives: cloud, tree, sun, moon, heart, woe, glee' and went on to suggest that these tended to become 'counters used in little games of abstract thought'.[8] Manifestations of this have already been noted in relation to his Georgian nature poetry. In these later volumes the tendency is aggravated by the demands of the subject matter. To register, even approximately, the mystical experience he needs images that suggest flight, levitation, extraterrestrial experiences. A word-count of these two volumes would reveal an abounding imagery of birds, clouds, moons, suns, leaves, buds, blossoms, winds, and on the other hand a succession of nouns which suggest or reflect spiritual states of consciousness and being such as dream, sleep, reverie, gloom, gleam, light, dark. Thus the deity moves

> From dream of dark to dream of light,
> From dream of naught to dream of all,
> He goes, nor aught relinquisheth,
> Dreaming a dream perpetual.[9]

And the albatross, type for the soul in search of nirvana:

> The wing that bears the albatross
> Over the gulf that he would cross
> Is kingly: royal, too, the eye
> Staring the utter deep and high,
> The void and monstrous steep of sky.[10]

The final difficulty that the poet encounters, and for which he does not find a satisfactory answer, is the semantic one. In an otherwise impressive poem, 'Kings and Tanists',[11] which explores the kingship of man in his curious role between the brute and the spirit Stephens progressively dismisses all the received notions of wisdom in favour of what might be called the kingdom of nothingness, which is the spirit. In its second movement, 'King with Herald', he writes

> —The good,
> The beautiful,
> The true—
> All that was learned
> In diligence, and pain,
> And taught, in trust, to you,
> Dismiss
> All this,
> For this is worthless all,
> And hath no act,
> And cometh not to call.

and proceeds to what one can only see as an irresolvable contradiction :

> Now welcome Doubt,
> Who searcheth all things out,
> And questions everything :
> Best friend of truth,
> And Herald of the King,
> And who will not be passed
> Of anything :

But if the 'true' is already declared worthless 'the truth' can have no recognisable status. It may be possible to interpret such passages as this—and there are several—in a more radical way, to argue that the poet is enacting a verbal drama that is meant to show, as in Beckett, the final exhaustion of language. But the interpretation is impossible to sustain in the light of the poems that come, before and after 'Kings and Tanists'. 'Theme and Variations', to take but one instance, ends affirmatively, if feebly with the lines :

The Good, the Beautiful, the True
Is Love,
And Loving,
And is you.

And furthermore the act of poetry remains throughout these volumes the chief human activity which can 'Banish the brute from off the man' and bring the soul to transcendent unity with the absolute.

'That Whereby a Poem is Wrought'

In an essay published in 1928 Stephens sets out his ideas on poetry, and describes his own experience of composition. He argues that 'poetry is closer to speech than prose is', because it is 'created in the whole phrase' while 'prose must be invented from comma to comma.' In his view poetry is 'a magical act' which comes mysteriously and involuntarily to the poet's consciousness: 'nothing in the nature of thinking had part in the birth or even the maturing of a poem. There was a feeling of intense, living activity; and this feeling, if it was not joy, certainly neighboured it.' This feeling which would last for two or three days was followed by 'a sort of rhythmic movement in the mind . . . still unconnected with words or thought'.

> A line of words came thereafter, appearing, as it seemed, from nowhere; and around and about that line the rhythm I speak of disported itself, swinging on it and around it as an acrobat swings on a trapeze; this rhythm was shaping the line certainly but it was as yet making no effort to add another line to it. . . . That line is the creative act made manifest. The rest of the poem lies in the will to continue it, or in the will to continue in the state from which it sprang.[12]

The concept of poetry proposed here is essentially inspirational and it accords with his view of the poetic act as expounded in several poems on the subject. The most powerful of these poetic excogitations is also among his most distinguished poems, 'The Pit of Bliss', first published in 1922. It may be read as a transitional poem recalling his early lyric practice—when he 'dared to sing / Of everything and anything'—and looking forward to his last poems where he consistently strives for nirvana—'Being

past all earthly cloy / And intermixture.' The poem's structure
enacts a determined progress in the definition of this state in
which the soul is made one with the Demiurge, the ultimate
source of its inspiration.

Having set up the co-ordinates of his meditation in the first
stanza the poet proceeds in the second to identify the moment of
spiritual intensity out of which the creative impulse is born:

> There is a Light
> Shines in the head:
> It is not gold,
> It is not red,
> But, as the lightning's blinding light,
> It is a stare of silver white . . .

This experience of light and colour—which is so prevalent in the
symbolism of the later poetry—is followed by the first voluntary
motion of creating mind:

> On that, mind-blinding, hue I gaze
> An instant, and am in a maze
> Of thinking—could one call it so?
> It is not thinking that I know!
> —An hurricane of Knowing, that
> Could whelm the soul . . .

In the third stanza the poet's sense of ecstasy finds its figurative
equivalent in the flight of an eagle in strenuous conflict with
the element which at once supports and masters it:

> An Eagle
> Whirling up the sky;
> Sunblind! Dizzy!
> Urging high,
> And higher beating yet a wing,
> Until he can no longer cling,
> Or hold; or do a thing, but fall,
> And sink, and whirl, and scream, through all
> His dizzy, heaven-hell of Pit,
> In mile-a-minute flight from it
> That he had dared! From height of height,
> So the Poet takes his flight

And tumble in the Pit of Bliss!
And, in the roar of that Abyss,
And falling, he will Sing and Sing
Of Everything, and Anything.

The eagle marks the climax of the poem: its aspiration and fall
symbolise the poet's struggle with the main force of his inspiration. The last stanza subsides into a cooler, more definitive
idiom: the language, carefully balanced between image and concept, registers the mood in which the illumination can reconstitute itself in poetry:

What is Knowing?
'Tis to see!
What is Feeling?
'Tis to be.
What is Love? But, more and more
To See and Be! To be a Pour
And avalanche of Being, till
Being ceases, and is still
For every motion—What is Joy?
—Being past all earthly cloy
And intermixture! Being spun
Of itself is Being won!
That is Joy—and this is God,
To be That, in cloud and clod:
And in cloud, and clod, to Sing
Of Everything, and Anything!

It is Stephens's most satisfying poem on the theme of poetic
creation. Despite the intractability of the language it must employ, especially the conceptual language of the last stanza, it
achieves a convincing statement of the creative process. The consistency of its stanzaic form, and the rhythmic vigour of its
metre, control and shape the ardour and ecstasy of its affirma-
tions. The abstract formulations of the final movement have been
earned in the metaphorical force of its two central stanzas.

'The Pit of Bliss' celebrates the primacy of spirit over 'earthly
cloy', yet it insists on the validity of the external world of 'cloud
and clod' as a theme for poetry. His subsequent treatments tend
to regard the material world as increasingly less worthy of the

poet's attention and to see the poet's active human capacities—
intellect, imagination, emotion, feeling, skill—as less and less
relevant to the creative act. In 'The Demiurge' he writes :

> Imagination does but seem :
> Thought is wisdom in a dream :
> And Emotion can, with pain,
> Tell a pleasure from a pain :
>
> These, the Sleepy Ones and Dull,
> That nothing sow, that nothing cull,
> Nothing have that's fit to sing
> The Wide Awake, the Living Thing.

Instead he proposes the 'living, ever-waking Will' as the sole
source of poetry, it being the faculty least encumbered with
matter, most neutral, most independent of the senses. The purpose
of poetry is now solely the celebration of 'the Living Thing', the
Oversoul; the will, offering itself in surrender to the Absolute,
becomes all-sufficient for the creative act :

> All that is not dull and dense,
> Bogged in thought, and clogged in sense,
> Comes unbid, and surge on surge,
> From the Will, the Demiurge.

Inevitably the poetry that issues from this new aesthetic virtually
abandons the world of the senses and contracts around the single,
elusive concept of nirvana, with the loss of concreteness and
visual imagery already noticed.

Ironically the one theme that retains its vitality is that of
poetic inspiration itself, and of the poet's consequent role as
mediator between time and eternity. The 'Theme' in 'Theme and
Variations' is introduced with a striking metaphor which recalls
at once Plato, the Vedas, Wordsworth's 'everlasting sea' and
Yeats's *anima mundi* :

> Thoughts will bubble up, and break,
> Spilling a sea, a limpid lake,
> Into the soul; and, as they go
> —Lightning visitors ! we know
> A lattice opened, and the mind
> Poised for all that is behind
> The lattice, and the poising mind.

Could the memory but hold!
—All the sunsets, flushed with gold,
Are streaming in it!

All the store
Of all that ever was before
Is teeming in it!

All the wit
Of holy living, holy writ,
Waiting till we remember it,
Is dreaming in it!

This image of the poetic act and the magic casements that it opens launches the poem on its twenty-four variations, all of which, with very uneven success, explore the relation between soul and body, spirit and oversoul, earth and heaven, time and eternity. The soul's fusion with the Absolute becomes, in the nineteenth 'Variation' a poetic act of transmuting:

Finding, unhid, the magic rod
That charms the brute into the god;
Raising the living from the dead,
Drawing, as from reluctant lead,
The gold of being, godlihead.

And in the twenty-first the poet's transfiguring power is asserted in a return of that concrete imagery which has become so rare in these later poems:

He hath the same dull eyes: his ears
Are dull attuned: his hopes and fears
Are those same ravening dogs that bay
The moon, and bury bones in clay!
Tho' he on offals, too, was bred,
Tho' in his heart, and in his head,
The brute doth slaver, yet he can
Banish the brute from off the man,
The man from that beyond the man.

The passage is startling not only in the context of the poem but in the context of the poet's entire work. The poem, despite the fugal ambition indicated in its title, does not achieve a formal coherence. Its recurrent images of star, lightning, leaf, bird, sun, moon, sea, sky, gold, rose, blossom, and its repeated motifs of transfiguration, are defeated by the looseness of its structure. The preponderance of abstract concepts, the archaisms, the hackneyed diction of religious awe and reverence, the apparent randomness with which the transitions are made from one lyric to the next, all conspire to create an impression of whimsicality and arbitrariness. But the raw force and energy of this short passage together with the precision of its imagery serve to enforce the essential seriousness of the poet's enterprise. The poem is about the tense duality of man's nature, the conflicting importunities of the flesh and the spirit. Situated as it is in the poem's sequence the passage provides a powerful retrospect, a backward pressure, in the reader's mind, and gives a renewed substantiality to the earlier less concrete formulations of the theme. Viewed in the larger perspectives of Stephens's work the passage calls to mind the persistence with which this tension of flesh and spirit has been explored and expounded through his writing career—in the early visionary poems, in the allegorical patterns of the prose fantasies, in the sexual tensions of the short stories, even in the psychological drama of the mythological redactions. The brute within and beneath the man, the god within and beyond the man, the drama of this conflict and its resolution has always been at the core of Stephens's concern. In these two final volumes of poetry, *Strict Joy* and *Kings and the Moon* the resolution is achieved. The soul must detach itself from the limitation of flesh, poetry must aspire towards the one transcendent reality, towards

> The One,
> The Witness,
> Knower of the Plot!
>
> Who bears life
> As a mask
> Upon a face,
>
> He goeth not!

The poetic implications of this final conviction—the last 'Variation' of the poem—are momentous for Stephens. The dramatic 'Plot' of human doubt and aspiration has reached its conclusion. The debate has come to rest in spiritual certainty. The Absolute has finally laid complete and proprietorial hold upon the poetic faculty. Only nirvana is worthy of the poetic exertion, and these last two books are almost exclusively deployed in its discovery and celebration. The game of material existence is no longer worth the candle. In giving his total allegiance to the Absolute the poet has in a literal sense gained his own soul but suffered the loss of the whole world. It is probably a consequent truth that poetry, when it is placed exclusively at the service of a reality external to itself, loses much of its intrinsic urgency. Beyond Nothingness there is only silence. In the last ten years of his life Stephens seems to have written no more than ten poems.

Conclusion

The enabling conviction behind this book is that James Stephens
was an artist, that he was, in Eliot's phrase, a writer who conducted a consistent 'raid upon the inarticulate'. He was never
a mere professional, that is a writer who discovers early a skill
and capacity to write within one or two literary *genres* and
exercises that skill and capacity without evincing any ambition
to find or create new patterns in form or language to explore
new areas of experience and sensibility. The artist is not necessarily greater than the professional but he is a different kind of
writer. In terms of greatness Trollope is closer to Joyce than
Stephens is. But Joyce and Stephens are artists in a radical sense
which sets them in a class apart from Trollope.

It is the mark of the artist that he is never content to repeat
himself. The same body of experience may furnish the material
for each new enterprise, but it is forever being re-shaped in terms
of a new form. The material of the first three stories of *Dubliners*
appears in *A Portrait of the Artist as a Young Man* but in a
radically different form. The material of the remainder, even its
dramatis personae, reappears in *Ulysses*, but there it has gone
through the sea-change of mythic transformation. The new possibilities for the novel created in *Ulysses*, under Joyce's demonic
obsession with form, are pushed to more radical extremes in the
verbal phantasmagoria of *Finnegans Wake*. Frank O'Connor's
impatience with Joyce, in his study of the short story in *The
Lonely Voice*, is the dismay of a great professional with a great
artist who refuses to rest in a medium which he has provisionally
mastered.

To be known solely as the writer of *The Crock of Gold* has
done Stephens a double disservice. It has led to his other prose
fantasies being dismissed out of hand as imperfect attempts to

produce a similar performance for an expectant market. Thus their radical experimentation has been ignored. Furthermore the 'Irish' aura of *The Crock of Gold* seen together with the leprecaun personality of its author has tended to obscure the modern and universal quality of both man and fable. Stephens has become therefore identified with what Patrick Kavanagh derisively termed 'the Irish Thing'. Thus, as a poet, it has become fashionable to dismiss him, together with Padraic Colum and F. R. Higgins, as one of AE's 'singing birds' whom the literary inflation of the Irish Literary Renaissance had overvalued.

These literary prejudices have unjustly masked the fact that Stephens was an artist of the utmost individuality whose life was a persistent, arduous and frequently brilliant experiment with experience and form. It has equally trivialised his deep spiritual seriousness, his unremitting struggle to resolve the mystery of existence through a lifetime of imaginative inquiry. And it has unfairly attributed an Irish provincialism to a writer whose work drew so heavily on universal sources even when the prism through which his vision was refracted happened to be overtly Irish.

His most impressive work is in the area of prose narrative. Here his mythic imagination and his narrative inventiveness achieved a series of remarkably original fictions. In an age which distrusts whimsy it is unfortunate but understandable that the surface charm and playfulness of the books have often deflected serious readers from the visionary seriousness at their centre. This vision was always radical and frequently subversive if seen against the social, political and religious background of its time. As archetypal human drama it has lost none of its relevance with the passing decades : the sense of human psychology that it enacts is independent of time and will respond with equal relevance to a Freudian or a Jungian exegesis. Stephens's experiment with different time-scales, his mock heroic treatment of the heroic and the mythic, his mixing of realism and fantasy, and his development of reflexive narrative techniques have all proven fruitful in the work of subsequent Irish novelists, Joyce, Eimar O'Duffy, Austin Clarke, Flann O'Brien and Benedict Kiely in particular.

His progress as a poet is, as has been acknowledged, less assured and consistent. But out of the body of his verse the finer dramatic lyrics, the best of the vision poems, the bulk of the Irish translations and a handful of the mystical poetry from his final period deserve to endure. The fact that his collected poems remain in print regardless of critical neglect is evidence enough of his authenticity as a poet.

The entire curve of his career reveals above all an impressive witness to the writer's vocation and a genuine exertion of the creative vision in a striking variety of literary forms.

Notes

INTRODUCTION (pp. ix–xii)

1. 'An Essay in Cubes', *English Review*, Vol. 17, April/July 1914.
2. *James, Seumas and Jacques*, ed. Lloyd Frankenberg, London: Macmillan, 1964, p. 90.
3. *The Letters of James Stephens*, ed. Richard J. Finneran, London: Macmillan, 1974, p. 140.
4. *James Stephens, a Literary and Bibliographical Study*, Dublin: Hodges and Figgis, 1959, p. 15.
5. *James Stephens*, London: Routledge and Kegan Paul, 1965, p. 4.
6. 'The Novelist and Final Utterance', *The Irish Statesman*, 2 April 1924.
7. *Letters*, p. 207.

CHAPTER 1 *THE CHARWOMAN'S DAUGHTER* (pp. 1–13)

1. James Stephens: *The Charwoman's Daughter*, Dublin: Gill and Macmillan, 1972, Chapter 20, p. 72.
2. *The Charwoman's Daughter*, Chapter 4, p. 20.
3. Ibid., Chapter 10.
4. *James Stephens, a Selection*, ed. Lloyd Frankenberg, London: Macmillan, 1962, p. 406.

CHAPTER 2 THE EARLY POETRY (pp. 14–37)

1. The second edition of Stephens's *Collected Poems* (1954) includes these two volumes as they had been published together with the poems written between 1938 and his death in 1950.
2. As these poems are scattered through the *Collected Poems* under thematic headings it will be helpful to list their titles and page numbers here, in the order of their mention: 'The Dancer' (79), 'The Red-Haired Man's Wife' (73), 'What Tomas Said in a Pub' (129), 'Fifty Pounds a Year and a Pension' (209), 'Where the Demons Grin' (157), 'Ould Snarly Gob' (163), 'Fossils' (70),

'What the Tramp Said' (212), 'To the Four Courts, Please' (206), 'A Street' (208).

3. Harold Bloom, *Yeats*, Oxford University Press, 1970, p. 5.
4. *The Irish Digest*, November 1950, pp. 50–2.
5. *Letters*, p. 111.
6. T. S. Eliot, *Prufrock and Other Concerns*, 1917; *Collected Poems*, London : Faber and Faber, 1963, p. 25.
7. His only significant comment on Pound is in a letter to *The New Age*, 18 March 1915 (*Letters*, p. 155), in which he accuses God of making 'policemen's feet to beat in the verse of Ezra Pound'. In the same letter he insists that 'we refer Mr Joyce's verse to his prose'. In a letter to Dilys Powell as late as 1934 he writes of Eliot 'I am not in sympathy with his verse', *Letters*, p. 386.
8. 'To the Four Courts, Please', C.P., p. 206.
9. The personae who made up part of Yeats's 'Phantasmagoria' (see 'A General Introduction to my Work', *Essays and Introductions*, London : Macmillan, 1961) were, in the early years, remote and esoteric personages—Robartes, Aherne, Hanrahan, Fergus, Cuchulain. It is in his later work, with the invention of Crazy Jane, that he employs the sort of earthy, profane and subversive persona which Stephens favoured in the dramatic lyrics of his first years.
10. This version is from *The Hill of Vision*. In the *Collected Poems* Stephens wisely left both concluding lines to the old woman, with a further gain in objectivity.
11. *Letters*, p. 216.
12. '*Tomas an Buile*' is ungrammatical Irish for 'Mad Thomas'. It ought to read either 'Tomas na Buile' or 'Tomas ar Buile'. In the *Collected Poems* the difficulty is evaded by a change of title to 'What Tomas Said in a Pub' on page 129.
13. Keynes, *Blake*, p. 185.
14. This title is excluded from his *Collected Poems*. In a letter to Thomas Bodkin in 1914 he regrets having dedicated it to Stephen MacKenna : 'Whenever I think of poor Stephen MacKenna I blush to think that I saddled my friend with that idiotic "Lonely God".'
15. Published in *Songs from the Clay* (1915), republished in *Collected Poems* under the title, 'The Devil' (p. 150).
16. *The Hill of Vision*, p. 76, *Collected Poems*, p. 143.
17. The phrase 'heels and head' (perhaps a wry pun on 'Hell and Heaven') is adopted for the title of Book Four of the *Collected Poems* in which these visionary poems are arranged together.
18. In 'A Vision of the Last Judgment' (Keynes, p. 617), Blake

wrote : ' "When the Sun rises, do you not see a round disk of fire somewhat like a Guinea?" O, no, no, no, I see an Innumerable company of the Heavenly host crying "Holy, Holy, Holy is the Lord Almighty." I question not my Corporeal and Vegetative Eye and more than I would question a Window concerning a Sight. I look thro' it and not with it.'

19. *Collected Poems*, p. 161.
20. Northrop Frye, *Fearful Symmetry*, Boston : Beacon Press, 1962, pp. 7–8.
21. *Letters*, pp. 145–6.
22. *James, Seumas, and Jacques*, London : Macmillan, 1964, p. 197.
23. 'Crionna' is the Irish for 'shrewd'; the poem, 'Nora Crionna' is in *Collected Poems*, p. 81.
24. *The Demi-Gods*, pp. 67–8.
25. Ibid., pp. 98–107.
26. Keynes, *Blake*, 'Jerusalem', 34, 15, p. 660.
27. Ibid., p. 739.
28. There may be an echo of Blake's Oothoon and Bromion 'Bound back to back' in 'Visions of the Daughters of Albion'.
29. Stephens may have in mind the oft-quoted dictum of the Smaragdine Tablet that earthly things are reflections of heavenly. This remark, beloved both by theosophists and kabbalists, is rendered by Yeats in 'Ribh Denounces Patrick' : 'For things below are copies, the Great Smaragdine Tablet said.'
30. See H. P. Blavatsky, *The Secret Doctrine*, London, 1893, vol. II, pp. 36–7.

CHAPTER 3 *THE CROCK OF GOLD* (pp. 38–55)
1. The author's note on the flyleaf of a first edition of the book, quoted in Bramsbäck, p. 134.
2. Reprinted in *Mythologies*, London, 1959.
3. *Studies,* Dublin, Spring 1975, 'Apocalyptic Structure in Yeats's Secret Rose'.
4. Schiller, *Essays Aesthetical and Philosophical*, 'On Simple and Sentimental Poetry', 1875.
5. *Letters*, p. 207.
6. Keynes, *Blake*, 'A Vision of the Last Judgment', 71–2, p. 605.
7. Alan Denson, ed., *Letters from A.E.*, London, 1961.
8. There is a full account of the cult of Celtic Paganism in Richard Ellmann's book, *Yeats: The Man and the Masks* in the chapter, 'Search for Unity'.
9. Mircea Eliade, *Myths, Dreams and Mysteries*, London : Collins, 1960, pp. 27–35.

10. The specific parody is of a passage in Act III of Synge's *Playboy*:
    Jimmy Farrell: I knew a party was kicked in the head by a red mare, and he went killing horses a great while, till he eat the insides of a clock and died after.
11. There is almost certainly an incidental parody of a poem by Padraic Colum here, 'The Old Woman of the Roads':
    Stephens: I wish to God I could get a cup of tea. . . . Me sitting down in my own little house, with the white table-cloth on the table, and the butter in the dish, and the strong, red tea in the teacup . . .
    Colum: Oh, to have a little house,
    To own the hearth and stool and all—
    The heaped-up sods upon the fire,
    The pile of turf against the wall! . . .
12. It seems certain that Stephens has in mind Blake's lines in 'Jerusalem', 56.16, referring to 'Non-Entity's dark wild', which was the destination of Thel when she recoiled from sexual fulfilment.
13. 'Jerusalem', Plate 49, 11.
    Learn therefore, O Sisters, to distinguish the Eternal Human,
    That walks about among the stones of fire in bliss & woe,
    Alternate, from those States or Worlds in which the Spirit travels,
    This is the only means to Forgiveness of Enemies.
14. *Crock*, Book VI, Chapter XVIII, p. 268. In Blake's view such forgiveness was necessary for the Brotherhood of man: cf. 'Jerusalem', Plate 96, 1.28 '. . . nor can Man exist but by Brotherhood'.
15. The Fomor, or Fomorians, were the mythical Irish tribe, ruled over by Balor of the Evil Eye, who were defeated by the Tuatha de Danann—the Shee, of whom Angus was one—at the Battle of Moytura. They can be seen as Stephens's Celtic equivalent of Urizen and his forces.
16. Hilary Pyle, *James Stephens, His Work and an Account of his Life*, London: Routledge and Kegan Paul, 1965, pp. 52–5.

CHAPTER 4 THE STEPHENS SHORT STORY (pp. 56–72)
1. He becomes 'The Old Gentleman' in *Here Are Ladies* and 'The Philosopher' in *The Crock of Gold*.
2. James Stephens, *The Crock of Gold*, London: Macmillan, 1912.

3. Birgit Bramsbäck, *James Stephens*, a Literary and Bibliographical Study, Dublin : Hodges and Figgis, 1959.
4. Ibid., see p. 45.
5. *Here Are Ladies*, p. 38.
6. Like the end of *The Crock of Gold* this is a variant on the 'apocalyptic' ending found in Yeats : instead of a change in the hero it implies a change in the world. But, whereas it is successful within the fantasy of *The Crock of Gold*, it collides with the realism of 'The Horses'.
7. *Etched in Moonlight*, p. 10.
8. 'James Stephens, Dublin-Paris Return', *The Colby Library Quarterly*, March 1961, p. 224.
9. James Stephens, *In the Land of Youth*, London : Macmillan, 1924, Part II.
10. *Etched in Moonlight*, p. 128.
11. James Esse, *Hunger*, a Dublin Story, Dublin : The Candle Press, 1918.
12. 'Come off that Fence', *The Irish Worker*, 13 Dec. 1913, p. 1.
13. *Etched in Moonlight*, p. 25.
14. Lloyd Frankenberg, *James Stephens, a Selection*, London : Macmillan, 1962, p. xxxi.

CHAPTER 5 *THE DEMI-GODS* (pp. 73–88)
1. Benedict Kiely, *Modern Irish Fiction*, Dublin, 1950, p. 71.
2. *Letters*, p. 17.
3. Ibid., pp. 19–20.
4. *The Secret Doctrine*, vol. I, p. 120.
5. Keynes, *Blake*, p. 669, 'Jerusalem', 41, illustration.
6. *The Secret Doctrine*, vol. i, p. 62.
7. According to Theosophy the soul of man passes through seven phases in its journey towards perfection. The ordinary human phase is the fourth. If it fails after death to ascend to the fifth phase, because of some karmic imperfection, it is thrown back into an earlier phase and has to renew the ascent. Art had expected that Brien O'Brien would have been more severely punished : 'I had expected him to be no more than one of the higher animals, or even that he might have been dissipated completely from existence.'
8. *Metamorphosis*, a study of the background and interpretation of vision in AE and James Stephens, by Mary Lorraine Weir, National University of Ireland, University College, Dublin, September 1968.

CHAPTER 6 GEORGIAN PASTORAL AND CHILDHOOD EPIPHANY (pp. 89–105)

1. Entitled 'Stephen's Green' in *Seamus Beg* (1915).
2. The poem appears in *Collected Poems* under the same title on p. 16 with a number of minor changes.
3. There is an able defence of the Georgian school in C. K. Stead's *The New Poetic*, Chapter 3, Pelican Books, 1964, and another in James Reeves's Introduction to the *Penguin Book of Georgian Poetry*, 1962.
4. Published by the Cultural Relations Committee, Dublin : Sign of the Three Candles, 1961, p. 20.
5. Title of the second section of *The Adventures of Seumas Beg*.
6. Ralph Hodgson, *Collected Poems*, London : Macmillan, 1961, p. 66.
7. Russell's parody of Stephens's light verse is unexpectedly shrewd :
   > Words themselves will multiply
   > With no guidance of the mind
   > High and sky and I and my
   > Easily beget their kind,
   > All that rhymes with high and dry
   > Flows with ceaseless fluency.
8. Ralph Hodgson, *Collected Poems*, Macmillan, 1961.
9. Collected Poems, p. 23. First published in *Little Things and Other Poems*, privately, 1924.
10. 'Reflections on Contemporary Poetry', *The Egoist*, September 1917.
11. *Letters*, p. 179.
12. *Collected Poems*, p. 167.
13. Especially 'An Encounter' where the hero meets the elderly and sinister fantast. The similarity is stronger, as will be seen, in another Seumas Beg epiphany, 'Behind the Hill'.
14. Robert Farren, *The Course of Irish Verse*, Sheed and Ward, 1948, p. 111.
15. *Collected Poems*, p. 176.

CHAPTER 7 STEPHENS AND THE EASTER RISING (pp. 106–113)

1. *Letters*, pp. 153–4.
2. Published originally by Maunsel, Dublin, 1916. Republished in paperback by Scepter, Dublin, 1966.

CHAPTER 8 *REINCARNATIONS* (pp. 114–125)

1. This poem is excluded from the *Collected Poems*—it is not very good—but its title is transferred to a poem which had been entitled 'Owen O'Neill' in *Reincarnations* and which now appears as 'The Land of Fal' on page 202 of *Collected Poems*.
2. *Letters*, pp. 232–3.

CHAPTER 9 MYTH, WONDER-TALE AND EPIC (pp. 126–147)

1. *Letters*, p. 61.
2. Ibid, pp. 240–1.
3. Ibid, 249.
4. *Explorations*, London : Macmillan, 1962, p. 333.
5. *Letters*, p. 277.
6. *The Candle of Vision*, re-published, Wheaton, Ill., U.S.A., 1965, p. 163.
7. Dublin : Maunsel, 1912.
8. *In the Land of Youth*, p. 109.
9. See *Irish Sagas*, ed. Myles Dillon, Dublin, Stationery Office, 1959, pp. 12–13.
10. 'The Adventures of Art Son of Conn', Eriu III, transl. R.I. Best.
11. Eleanor Hull, *The Cuchullin Saga*, London : David Nutt, 1898.
12. Standish H. O'Grady, *Silva Gadelica*, London, 1892, p. 383.
13. *In the Land of Youth*, pp. 104, 105.
14. T. P. Cross and C. H. Slover, *Ancient Irish Tales*, Dublin : Allen Figgis, 1969, p. 241.
15. 'Literary Treatment of the Deirdre Legend' by Roger McHugh, *Threshold*, vol. I, No. 1, February 1957.
16. *Deirdre*, Chapter IV.

CHAPTER 10 THEME AND VARIATIONS (pp. 148–159)

1. *Letters*, p. 350.
2. *Collected Poems*, p. 287.
3. *Letters*, p. 343.
4. *Collected Poems*, p. 254. First published in *A Poetry Recital*, 1926.
5. *Letters*, p. 277.
6. Published in *Collected Poems*, p. 255, under the title 'Thy Soul'.
7. *Collected Poems*, p. 307.
8. *Times Literary Supplement*, 20 July 1962, p. 526.
9. 'Theme and Variations' from *Strict Joy*, *Collected Poems*, p. 286.
10. Ibid., p. 287.

11. From *Kings and the Moon, Collected Poems*, pp. 311–22.
12. The essay was first published by the Bowling Green Press, New York, 1928, and is republished in Frankenberg, pp. 399–412.

SELECT BIBLIOGRAPHY

James Stephens

For an exhaustive list of Stephens's publications the authoritative sources are Bramsbäck's *James Stephens* (see below, General References) and Finneran's *Letters*, Appendix B, which includes additional material partly drawn from intermediate research by Richard Cary, Lloyd Frankenberg and Hilary Pyle. The following is confined to the main publications in their Irish, British and American editions.

Insurrections, Dublin : Maunsel, 1909. New York : Macmillan, 1909.

The Hill of Vision, Dublin : Maunsel, 1912. New York : Macmillan, 1912.

The Charwoman's Daughter, London : Macmillan, 1912. American title, *Mary Mary*, Boston : Small, Maynard, 1912.

The Crock of Gold, London : Macmillan, 1912. New York : Macmillan, 1913.

Here Are Ladies, London : Macmillan, 1913. New York : Macmillan, 1913.

The Demi-Gods, London : Macmillan, 1914. New York, Macmillan, 1914.

Songs from the Clay, London : Macmillan, 1915. New York : Macmillan, 1915.

The Adventures of Seumas Beg and The Rocky Road to Dublin, London : Macmillan, 1915. New York : Macmillan, 1915.

Green Branches, Dublin : Maunsel, 1916. New York : Macmillan, 1916.

The Insurrection in Dublin, Dublin : Maunsel, 1916. New York : Macmillan, 1916.

Reincarnations, London : Macmillan, 1918. New York : Macmillan, 1918.

Irish Fairy Tales, London : Macmillan, 1920. New York : Macmillan, 1920.

Deirdre, London : Macmillan, 1923. New York : Macmillan, 1923.

In the Land of Youth, London : Macmillan, 1924. New York : Macmillan, 1924.

Collected Poems, London : Macmillan, 1926. New York : Macmillan, 1926.

Etched in Moonlight, London : Macmillan, 1928. New York : Macmillan, 1928.

On Prose and Verse, New York : Bowling Green Press, 1928.

Julia Elizabeth, A Comedy in One Act (stage version of part I, 'Three Lovers who Lost' in *Here Are Ladies*), New York : Crosby Gaige, 1929.

Strict Joy, London : Macmillan, 1931. New York : Macmillan, 1931.

Kings and the Moon, London : Macmillan, 1938. New York : Macmillan, 1938.

James Stephens, a Selection, ed. Lloyd Frankenberg, London : Macmillan, 1962.

James, Seumas and Jacques, ed. Lloyd Frankenberg, London : Macmillan, 1964. New York : Macmillan, 1964.

Letters of James Stephens, ed. Richard Finneran, London and New York : Macmillan, 1974.

GENERAL REFERENCES

Blake, William, *Complete Writings*, ed. Sir Geoffrey Keynes, London : O.U.P., 1972.

Blavatsky, H. P. B., *The Secret Doctrine*, London : Theosophical Publishing Co., 1888.

Bloom, Harold, *Yeats*, London : O.U.P., 1970.

Boyd, Ernest, *Ireland's Literary Renaissance*, Dublin : Allen Figgis, 1968.

Bramsbäck, Birgit, *James Stephens, a Literary and Bibliographical Study*, Dublin : Hodges and Figgis, 1959.

Brown, Stephen J., *Ireland in Fiction, a Guide to Irish Novels, Tales, Romances, Folk-lore*, Dublin and London : Maunsel, 1919.

Clarke, Austin, *Poetry in Modern Ireland*, Dublin : Cultural Relations Committee, Sign of the Three Candles, 1961.

Clarke, Austin, *The Bright Temptation*, Dublin : Dolmen, 1965.

Clarke, Austin, *The Singing Men at Cashel*, London : Allen and Unwin, 1936.

Clarke, Austin, *The Sun Dances at Easter*, London : Melrose, 1952.

Colum, Padraic, *The King of Ireland's Son*, New York : Macmillan, 1916.

Colum, Padraic, *The Poet's Circuits*, London : O.U.P., 1960.

Cross, T. P. and Slover, C. H., *Ancient Irish Tales*, New York : Harrap, 1936.

Eliade, Mircea, *Myths, Dreams and Mysteries*, London, Collins (Fontana), 1968.

Farren, Robert, *The Course of Irish Verse*, London : Sheed and Ward, 1948.

Finneran, Richard G., McFate, Patricia, eds., *The Journal of Irish Literature*, a James Stephens number, Vol. IV, No. 3, Sept. 1975.

Frye, Northrop, *Fearful Symmetry*, Boston : Beacon Press, 1947.

Frye, Northrop, *Anatomy of Criticism*, Princeton University Press, 1965.

Frye, Northrop, *Fables of Identity*, New York : Harcourt, Brace and World, 1963.

Gregory, Augusta Lady, *Gods and Fighting Men*, Gerrards Cross : Colin Smythe, 1970.

Gregory, Augusta, Lady, *Cuchulain of Muirtheimne*, Gerrards Cross : Colin Smythe, 1970.

Hodgson, Ralph, *Collected Poems*, London : Macmillan, 1961.

Hull, Eleanor, *A Text Book of Irish Literature*, Dublin : Gill, 1908.

Hull, Eleanor, *The Cuchullin Saga*, London : David Nutt, 1898.

Joyce, James, *Dubliners*, New York : Viking Critical, 1969.

Joyce, James, *Portrait*, New York : Viking Critical, 1968.

Joyce, James, *Ulysses*, London : Bodley Head, 1937.

Joyce, James, *Finnegans Wake*, London : Faber, 1964.

Joyce, P. W., *Old Celtic Romances*, Dublin : Talbot Press, 1961.

Kiely, Benedict, *Modern Irish Fiction*, Golden Eagle, 1950.

Kiely, Benedict, *The Cards of the Gambler* (novel), Dublin : Millington Press, 1973.

Kinsella, Thomas, *The Táin*, Dublin : Dolmen.

Leahy, A. H., *Heroic Romances of Ireland*, I and II, London, 1905, 1906.

McHugh, Roger, 'Literary Treatments of the Deirdre Legend', *Threshold*, Belfast, Vol. I, No. I, February 1957.

MacKenna, Stephen, *Plotinus*, Vols. I–II, London : Philip Lee Warner, 1917 (translation).

Martin, Augustine, 'The Secret Rose, Yeats's Dialogue with History', *Ariel* (Calgary), Vol. 3, No. 3, July 1972.

Martin, Augustine, 'Apocalyptic Structure in Yeats's *Secret Rose*' *Studies* (Dublin), Vol. LXIV, No. 253, Spring 1975.

Martin, Augustine, ed. with Introduction, *The Charwoman's Daughter*, Dublin : Gill and Macmillan, 1972.

Mercier, Vivien, 'James Stephens, his Versions of the Pastoral', *Irish Writing*, XIV, March 1951.

Mercier, Vivien, *The Irish Comic Tradition*, London : O.U.P., 1962.

Meyer, Kuno, *The Voyage of Bran*, London : David Nutt, 1895.

Murphy, Gerard, *Saga and Myth in Ancient Ireland*, Dublin : Cultural Relations Committee, The Sign of the Three Candles, 1955.

Murphy, Gerard, *Ossianic Lore and Romantic Tales of Medieval Ireland,* Dublin : Cultural Relations Committee, The Sign of The Three Candles, 1955.

O'Brien, Flann, *At Swim Two Birds,* London : Macgibbon and Kee, 1960.

O'Connor, Frank, *Kings, Lords and Commons,* London : Macmillan, 1961.

O'Duffy, Eimar, *King Goshawk and the Birds,* London : Macmillan, 1926.

O'Grady, Standish H., *Silva Gadelica,* London : Williams and Norgate, 1892.

O'Grady, Standish James, *History of Ireland,* Vols. I–II, London : 1878–80.

O'Grady, Standish James, *The Coming of Cuculain,* London : 1895.

O'Rahilly, Thomas Francis, *Early Irish History and Mythology,* Dublin : Institute of Advanced Studies, 1946.

Ó Súilleabháin, Seán, *Storytelling in Ireland,* Cultural Relations Committee, Mercier Press (Cork), 1973.

Propp, V., *The Morphology of the Folktale* (transl. Laurence Scott), Austin and London : University of Texas Press, 1968.

Pyle, Hilary, *James Stephens, his Work and an Account of his Life,* London : Routledge and Kegan Paul, 1965.

Russell, George (AE), *Letters from AE,* ed. Alan Denson, London : Abelard Schuman, 1961.

Russell, George (AE), *Collected Poems,* London : Macmillan, 1920.

Russell, George (AE), *The Candle of Vision,* Gerrards Cross : Colin Smythe, 1974.

Summerfield, Henry, *That Myriad-Minded Man,* Biography of AE, Gerrards Cross : Colin Smythe, 1975.

Wall, Mervyn, *The Unfortunate Fursey,* London : Pilot Press, 1946.

Wall, Mervyn, *The Return of Fursey,* London : Pilot Press, 1948.

Yeats, W. B., *Collected Poems,* London : Macmillan, 1950.

Yeats, W. B., *Collected Plays,* London : Macmillan, 1953.

Yeats, W. B., *A Vision,* New York : Macmillan, 1956.

Yeats, W. B., *Mythologies,* London : Macmillan, 1959.

Yeats, W. B., *The Secret Rose,* Dublin : Maunsel, 1905

Index